mu
San Francisco

Golden Gate Bridge viewed from Baker Beach at sunset, ©Stephan Hoerold/iStockphoto.com

mustsees **San Francisco**

Editorial Manager	Jonathan P. Gilbert
Editor	Craig Nelson
Principal Writer	Barbara Rockwell
Production Manager	Natasha G. George
Cartography	Peter Wrenn
Photo Editor	Yoshimi Kanazawa
Photo Research	Scott Sendrow,
Proofreaders	Scott Sendrow, Clive Hebard
Layout	Annika Jermyn, Eleanor Renée Rogers, Natasha G. George
Interior Design	Chris Bell, cbdesign
Cover Design	Chris Bell, cbdesign, Natasha G. George
Contact Us	Michelin Travel and Lifestyle
	One Parkway South
	Greenville, SC 29615
	USA
	www.michelintravel.com
	michelin.guides@us.michelin.com
	Michelin TravelPartner
	Hannay House
	39 Clarendon Road
	Watford, Herts WD17 1JA
	UK
	(01923) 205 240
	www.ViaMichelin.com
	travelpubsales@uk.michelin.com
Special Sales	For information regarding bulk sales, customized editions and premium sales, please contact our Customer Service Departments:
	USA 1-800-432-6277
	UK (01923) 205 240
	Canada 1-800-361-8236

Michelin Apa Publications Ltd

A joint venture between Michelin and Langenscheidt

58 Borough High Street, London SE1 1XF, United Kingdom

No part of this publication may be reproduced in any form without the prior permission of the publisher.

© 2011 Michelin Apa Publications Ltd
ISBN 978-1-907099-38-0
Printed: August 2011
Printed and bound: Himmer, Germany

Note to the reader:

While every effort is made to ensure that all information printed in this guide is correct and up-to-date, Michelin Apa Publications Ltd. accepts no liability for any direct, indirect or consequential losses howsoever caused so far as such can be excluded by law. Admission prices listed for sights in this guide are for a single adult, unless otherwise specified.

Peter Wrenn/Alamy

Alamo Square

Introduction

San Francisco:
Beauty By The Bay 20

Must See

p41

TABLE OF CONTENTS

★★★ ATTRACTIONS

Unmissable attractions awarded three stars in this guide include:

Golden Gate Park   p 68

©Daniella Nowitz/Apa Publications

Golden Gate Bridge   p 40

Regis Lefebure/SFCVB

Fisherman's Wharf   p 38

Jerry Lee Hayes/SFCVB

Alcatraz   p 36

Brigitta L. House/MICHELIN

MUST KNOW

Postcard Row p 43, 112

© Richard Nowitz/Apa Publications

Wine Country p 91

Brigitta L. House/MICHELIN

Coit Tower p 37

Mami Miyata/SFCVB

Chinatown p 22

Brigitta L. House/MICHELIN

STAR ATTRACTIONS

★★★ ATTRACTIONS

Unmissable sights in and around San Francisco

For more than 75 years people have used the Michelin stars to take the guesswork out of travel. Our star-rating system helps you make the best decision on where to go, what to do, and what to see.

★★★	Absolutely Must See
★★	Really Must See
★	Must See
No Star	See

★One-Star

🐻 ACTIVITIES

Unmissable Bars, Shows, Shopping and more
Look-out for the Michelin Man throughout the guide for the top activities.

🐻 Kids

🐻 Days Out

🐻 Food/Drink

🐻 Nightlife

🐻 Shopping

🐻 Hotels/Spas

STAR ATTRACTIONS

CALENDAR OF EVENTS

Listed below is a selection of San Francisco's most popular annual events. Please note that dates may change from year to year. For more detailed information, contact the San Francisco Convention and Visitors Bureau *(415-391-2000; www.onlyinsanfrancisco.com)*.

January

Chinese New Year Parade & Celebration
Chinatown
415-986-1370
www.chineseparade.com

February

Valentine's Day Woo at the Zoo
San Francisco Zoo
415-753-7165
www.sfzoo.org
San Francisco Beer Week
Various locations
www.sfbeerweek.org

March

San Francisco International Asian American Film Festival
Various venues
caamedia.org/festival
St. Patrick's Day Parade
Civic Center Plaza
www.UISSF.org

April

Cherry Blossom Festival
City Hall & Japantown
www.sfjapantown.org/Events/cherry.cfm
Spring Celebration & Easter Parade
Union St. between Gough & Fillmore Sts.
www.sresproductions.com
San Francisco International Film Festival
Various venues
415-561-5000
www.sffs.org

May

Bay to Breakers Race
Embarcadero to Great Highway
415-359-2800
www.carnavalsf.com

September Autumn Moon Festival, Chinatown

©Wing Cheng/SF Chinatown Merchants Association

MUST KNOW

Cinco de Mayo Festival
Mission District
415-826-1401

June
San Francisco Pride
Castro District
415-864-3733
www.sfpride.org
North Beach Festival
Grant Ave. & Green St.
415-989-2220
northbeachchamber.com
Union Street Festival
Union St. between
550-232-5030
Gough & Steiner Sts.
www.unionstreetfestival.com
Stern Grove Festival
Sigmund Stern Grove
(mid-June to mid-Aug)
415-252-6252
www.sterngrove.org

July
Fourth of July
Waterfront Festival
Fisherman's Wharf
415-705-5500
www.pier39.com
Midsummer Mozart Festival
Various venues
415-627-9142
www.midsummermozart.org
San Francisco Shakespeare Festival
Golden Gate Park (July–Oct)
415-558-0888
www.sfshakes.org

August
Outside Lands
Golden Gate Park
www.sfoutsidelands.com
Nihonmachi Street Fair
Japantown & Japan Center
415-771-9861
www.nihonmachistreetfair.org

September
Autumn Moon Festival
Chinatown
415-982-6306
www.moonfestival.org
Ghirardelli Chocolate Festival
Ghirardelli Square
415-775-5500
www.ghirardellisq.com
San Francisco Fringe Festival
Theater District
415-931-1094
www.sffringe.org
Sausalito Art Festival
Marinship Park
415-331-3757
www.sausalitoartfestival.org
Folsom Street Fair
South of Market
415-861-3247
www.folsomstreetfair.org
Opera in the Park
Golden Gate Park
sfopera.com

October
Fleet Week
Marina Green Park &
Fisherman's Wharf
650-599-5057
www.fleetweek.us
Italian Heritage Parade & Festival
North Beach
415-703-9888
www.sfcolumbusday.org
San Francisco Jazz Festival
Various locations
415-398-5655
www.sfjazz.org
Hardly Strictly Bluegrass Festival
Golden Gate Park
www.strictlybluegrass.com
Litquake
Various venues
415-750-1497
litquake.org

CALENDAR OF EVENTS

PLANNING YOUR TRIP

Before you go, contact the following agencies to obtain maps and information about sightseeing, accommodations, travel packages, recreational opportunities and seasonal events.

San Francisco Convention & Visitors Bureau – 900 Market St., San Francisco, CA 94102; *415-391-2000; www.onlyin sanfrancisco.com*

Visitors Information Center – **Located on the lower level of Hallidie Plaza Market & Powell Sts.;** Open Mon–Fri 5pm, Sun 9am-3pm *(closed on Sundays November through April); 415-391-2000*

Berkeley Convention & Visitors Bureau – 2030 Addison St., #102., Berkeley, CA 94704; *510-549-7040; www.visitberkeley.com; Open Mon-Fri 9am-1pm and 2pm-5pm (closed on holidays)*

Marin Convention & Visitors Bureau – 1 Mitchell Boulevard, Suite B;San Rafael, CA 94903; *415-925-2060; www. visitmarin.org; Open Mon–Thu 9am-5pm, Fri 9am-3pm*

Napa Valley Conference & Visitors Bureau – 1310 Napa Town Center, Napa, CA 94559; *707-226-5813x106; www.napavalley.org*

Oakland Convention & Visitors Bureau – 463 11th Street Oakland,

CA 94607; *510-839-9000; www.oaklandcvb.com*

San Mateo County Convention & Visitors Bureau – 111 Anza Blvd., Suite 410, Burlingame, CA 94010; *650-348-7600; www.sanmateo countycvb.com; Open Mon – Thu 8.30am-5pm Fri 8.30am-4pm*

Santa Rosa Convention & Visitors Bureau – 9 Fourth St., Santa Rosa, CA 95401; *707-577-8674; www.visitsantarosa.com; Mon–Sat 9am-5pm Sun 10am-5pm*

CityPass – Consider buying a CityPass booklet *($69, adults; $39 ages 5–11; good for 7 consecutive days),* which gives you substantially

In the News

San Francisco's main newspaper is the *San Francisco Chronicle* (*www.sfgate.com*). Its Sunday edition features an extensive arts-and-entertainment supplement.
The free *San Francisco Examiner* (*www.sfexaminer.com*) is published daily Sun–Fri and can be found at bookstores, cafes, and newspaper boxes around the city.
Two weekly alternative papers, *The San Francisco Bay Guardian* (*www.sfbg.com*) and the *SF Weekly* (*www.sfweekly.com*), both published on Wednesday, offer different perspectives of the city as well as diverse and comprehensive entertainment sections.

Average Seasonal Temperatures in San Francisco				
(recorded at SF Int'l Airport)				
	Jan	Apr	July	Oct
Avg. high	56°F / 13°C	64°F / 18°C	70°F / 22°C	70°F / 21°C
Avg. low	43°F / 6°C	48°F / 9°C	55°F / 13°C	52°F /11°C

discounted admission to the following attractions: Blue & Gold Fleet cruises, San Francisco Museum of Modern Art, California Academy of Sciences, Aquarium of the Bay, and either the Exploratorium or the Legion of Honor and de Young museums. Booklets also include a 7-day pass for MUNI public transportation and cable cars.

Buy your CityPass at the Visitor Information Center (above), at any of the participating attractions, or online at *www.citypass.com*.

TIPS FOR DISABLED VISITORS

Federal law requires that businesses (including hotels and restaurants) provide access for the disabled, devices for the hearing impaired, and designated parking spaces. For further information, contact the **Society for Accessible Travel and Hospitality (SATH),**

347 Fifth Ave., Suite 605, New York NY 10016 (212-447-7284; www.sath.org).
All national parks have facilities for the disabled, and offer free or discounted passes. For details, contact the **National Park Service** *(Office of Information) Room 1013, 1849 C St. NW, Washington, D.C. 20240; 202-208-4747; www.nps.gov).* Passengers who will need assistance with train or bus travel should give advance notice to **Amtrak** *(800-872-7245 or 800-523-6590/TDD; www.amtrak.com)* or **Greyhound** *(800-752-4841 or 800-345-3109/TDD; www.grey hound.com).* Reservations for hand-controlled rental cars should

Important Phone Numbers	
Emergency (24hrs)	✆ **911**
Police (non-emergency, Mon–Fri 9am–6pm)	✆ 415-553-0123
Poison Control	✆ 800-876-4766
Medical Referral:	
Travelers Medical Group (24hrs)	✆ 415-981-1102
SF On-Call	✆ 415-732-7029
Downtown Medical Travel Group	✆ 415-362-7177
Visitors Medical Services	✆ 415-353-6000
Dental Emergencies	✆ 415-421-1435
24-hour Pharmacies: Walgreens (800-289-2273)	
3201 Divisadero St., Marina District	✆ 415-931-6415
498 Castro St., Castro District	✆ 415 861-3136
Bay Area Transit Information Hotline: (within San Francisco)	✆ 511

PRACTICAL INFORMATION

be made in advance with the rental company.

Local Lowdown – The following publications provide detailed information about access for the disabled in San Francisco and Northern California:

Access Northern California – *(ANC, 1427 Grant St., Berkeley, CA 94703; 510-524-2026; www.accessnca.com).*

Access San Francisco – *(San Francisco Convention & Visitors Bureau; 415-391-2000 or 415-392-0328 TDD; www.sfvisitor. org).* If you're in town, pick up a copy of this publication at the Visitors Information Center located on the lower level of Hallidie Plaza (Market & Powell Sts.).

MUNI Access Guide – *(San Fran-cisco Municipal Railway; 415-701- 4485; TTY 415-701-4730; www.sfmuni.com).*

Senior Citizens – Many hotels, attractions and restaurants offer discounts to visitors age 62 or older (proof of age may be required).

The American Association of

Fog

It may roll in on little cat's feet, but San Francisco's fog can put a damper on your **sightseeing**—especially if you were planning on enjoying long-range views. When the fog sets in, temperatures drop suddenly, making a sweater or jacket necessary. **Spring** fogs occur in the early morning and generally lift by midday. In summer, fog can last all day by the coast, though it may burn off over inland areas before it comes back in the evening. **Autumn** days are relatively fog-free. Winter fogs usually occur inland, leaving coastal areas in the clear.

Retired Persons (AARP), *(601 E St. NW, Washington DC 20049; 888-687-2277; www.aarp.com)* offers discounts to its members.

WHEN TO GO

Sure, you've heard Mark Twain's jibe that the coldest winter he ever spent was a summer in San Francisco. Even so, the Bay Area enjoys a temperate climate year-round. Although temperatures vary little from season to season, weather conditions can change quite suddenly in the course of a day, and from area to area. Inland temperatures are generally higher than those along the windy oceanfront and the bay shore. The region's glorious views are at their finest during the clear days of autumn, when daytime temperatures in the 70s make for great sightseeing.

Rain is the norm during the winter months with more than 85% of the annual precipitation occurring between November and April, when temperatures hover between 45° and 60°F. The busiest tourist season is July and August; make advance reservations whenever possible and expect long lines for the more popular attractions.

GETTING THERE
By Air

San Francisco is served by two international airports:

San Francisco International Airport (SFO) – *13.5mi south of San Francisco via US-101 (650-821-8211; www.flysfo.com).*

Oakland International Airport (OAK) – *18mi east of San Francisco via I-80 and I-880 (510-563-3300; www.flyoakland.com).*

By Train

Emeryville is the home of the closest railroad station to San Francisco. Located across the bay, the station offers **Amtrak** and shuttling services *(5885 Landregan St.; 800-872-7245; www.amtrak.com)*.

By Bus

San Francisco's new **Transbay Transit Center** is scheduled to be completed in 2017.
In the interim, the Temporary Transbay terminal is located at the block bounded by Main, Folsom, Beale and Howard streets.
For ticketing information, visit www.temporaryterminal.org.

By Car

San Francisco can be easily accessed from a number of major highways. **I-280** enters the city from the south. **I-80** crosses the **Bay Bridge** from Berkeley and Oakland *($4-6 toll, varying by day and time)*. **US-101**, which enters San Francisco from the south, also provides access to the city from the north, crossing the **Golden Gate Bridge** *($6 toll for southbound traffic only)*.

GETTING AROUND
By Car

Driving can be a hassle in San Francisco, where the roads are congested and parking is difficult to find and often expensive.
Visitors are encouraged not to drive during commuter **rush hours** *(weekdays 7:30am-9am and 4pm-6pm)*. Cars are, however, useful for visiting surrounding areas such as the Wine Country and Marin County. Use of seat belts is required. Child safety seats are mandatory for children under 6 years and 60 pounds.
Parking – San Francisco's hills pose a special problem when you're

Car Rental		
Car Rental Company	**⟋ Reservations**	**Website**
Alamo	877-222-9075	www.alamo.com
Avis	800-230-4898	www.avis.com
Budget	800-527-0700	www.budget.com
Dollar	800-800-5252	www.dollar.com
Enterprise	800-261-7331	www.enterprise.com
Hertz	800-654-3131	www.hertz.com
National	877-222-9058	www.nationalcar.com
Thrifty	800-847-4389	www.thrifty.com

PRACTICAL INFORMATION

Cable Cars

What would a visit to San Francisco be without a ride on a cable car? Invented by **Andrew Smith Hallidie** in 1873, the city's signature public transportation system carries over 7 million passengers each year. Today, 40 cable cars operate along three lines: Powell-Hyde, Powell-Mason and California Street (daily 6am–1am). You can board a cable car about every 10 minutes at any stop (marked by brown signs) along the route. However, the cars tend to fill up as the day goes on, especially on weekends and in summer. You can pay on-board ($5 one way) or buy a book of tickets at the visitor information center located on Hallidie Plaza (900 Market St.). CityPass booklets include passes for BART and the cable cars. Ticket booths are located at Powell and Market streets and at Hyde and Beach streets (two ends of the line). MUNI passports for one ($13), three ($20), or 7 ($26) days are available at the Hallidie Plaza visitor center, at information booths at the airport or online at www. sfmta.com. To learn more about this unusual transportation system, visit the Cable Car Museum (1201 Mason St.; *see Museums*).

parking. When parking on a hill, be sure to turn the front wheels of your vehicle against the curb. Facing downhill, turn the wheels toward the curb; facing uphill, turn the wheels away from the curb. Needless, to say, the use of a parking brake is mandatory.

On Foot

Walking is one of the best ways to explore San Francisco—and a great way to get a workout. The city's Convention and Visitors Bureau lists a variety of walking tours on its Web site *(www.onlyinsanfrancisco.com)*. If you're planning to walk, it helps to know which streets are the steepest *(see list in Landmarks/Lombard Street)*.

By Public Transportation

The San Francisco Municipal Railway (MUNI) operates an extensive network of transportation lines using diesel and electric buses, light-rail streetcars and cable cars *(311; www.sfmta.com)*. Standard bus fare is $2 per ride. **Golden Gate Transit**

(415-455-2000; www.golden gatetransit.org) provides bus services to Marin, Contra Costa and Sonoma Counties; **SamTrans** *(510-817-1717; www.samtrans.com)* serves **San Mateo County**; and **AC Transit** *(511; www.actransit.org)* serves **Alameda and Contra Costa Counties**. *511.org* provides information for all transportation systems in the Bay Area.

The Bay Area Rapid Transit (BART) commuter rail line links San Francisco with cities in the East Bay *(see map above; 415-989-2278; www.bart.gov)*.

Fares are determined on a per-mileage basis. Trains operate Mon–Fri 4am–midnight, Sat 6am–midnight, Sun 8am–midnight.

By Taxi

All San Francisco taxicab companies share the same rate schedule: $3.10 for the first ⅕ mile and $0.45 for each additional ⅕ mile. Taxis may not be readily available; it's best to call for a pickup. Major cab companies in the city include **Yellow Cab** *(415-333-3333)*, **Luxor Cab** *(415-282-4141)* and **Desoto Cab** *(415-552-1300)*.

FOREIGN VISITORS

Visitors from outside the US can obtain information from the **San Francisco Convention and Visitors Bureau** *(415-391-2000; www.onlyinsanfrancisco.com)* or from the US embassy or consulate in their country of residence. For a list of Web sites of foreign embassies in the US, visit *http://www.state.gov/s/cpr/rls/dpl/32122.html.*

Entry Requirements

Travelers entering the United States under the **Visa Waiver Program (VWP)** must have a machine-readable passport. Any traveler without a machine-readable passport will be required to obtain a visa before entering the US. Citizens of VWP countries are permitted to enter the US for general business or tourist purposes for a maximum of 90 days without needing a visa.

Requirements for the Visa Waiver Program can be found at the **Department of State's Visa Services** Web site *(http://travel.state.gov/visa/visa_1750.html).* Residents of Visa Waiver countries must apply ahead for travel authorization online through the ESTA program *(www.cbp.gov/esta).* All citizens of non-participating countries must have a visitor's visa. Upon entry, nonresident foreign visitors must present a valid passport and round-trip transportation ticket.

Canadian citizens are not required to present a passport or visa, but they must present a valid photo ID and proof of citizenship. Naturalized Canadian citizens should carry their citizenship papers.

US Customs – All articles brought into the US must be declared at the time of entry. Prohibited items: plant material; firearms and

17

ammunition (if not for sporting purposes); meat or poultry products. For information, contact the **US Customs Service**, 1300 Pennsylvania Ave. NW, Washington DC 20229 *(202-354-1000; www.cbp.gov)*.

Money and Currency Exchange –Visitors can exchange currency at the **Thomas Cook Currency Services** *(2301 Shattuck Ave., Berkeley; 510-849-8520)*, **Bank of America** *(345 Montgomery St.; 415-622-8248)* or **American Express Travel Service** *(455 Market St.; 415-536-2600; http://www.amextravel resources.com)*. For cash transfers, **Western Union** *(800-325-6000; www.westernunion.com)* has agents throughout San Francisco. Banks, stores, restaurants and hotels accept travelers' checks with photo identification.

To report a lost or stolen credit card – **American Express** *(850- 882- 028)*; **Diners Club** *(800-234-6377)*; **MasterCard** *(800-627-8372)*; **Visa** *(800-847-2911)*.

Driving in the US

Visitors bearing **valid driver's licenses** issued by their country of residence are not required to obtain an International Driver's License. Drivers must carry vehicle registration and/or rental contract, and proof of automobile insurance at all times. **Gasoline** is sold by the gallon (1 gal=3.8 liters). Vehicles in the US are driven on the right-hand side of the road.

Electricity

Voltage in the US is 120 volts AC, 60 Hz. Foreign-made appliances may need AC adapters (available at specialty travel and electronics

stores) and North American flat-blade plugs.

Taxes and Tipping

Prices displayed in the US do not include the California sales tax of 9.25%, which is not reimbursable. It is customary to give a small gift of money—a tip—for services rendered, to waiters (18–20% of bill), porters ($1 per bag), chamber maids ($1-2 per day) and cab drivers (15% of fare).

Time Zone

San Francisco is in the Pacific Standard Time (PST) zone, eight hours behind Greenwich Mean Time, and three hours behind New York City.

ACCOMMODATIONS

For a list of suggested accommodations, *see Hotels*. An area visitors' guide including lodging directory is available (free) from the San Francisco Convention and Visitors Bureau. Hotel Reservation Services:

San Francisco Convention and Visitors Center – 888-782-9673
San Francisco Reservations – *800-677-1570*
Central Reservation Service – *800-555-7555*
Youth Hostels – *www.norcal hostels.org.* A no-frills, inexpensive alternative to hotels, hostels are a great choice for budget travelers. Prices average $25–$75 per night.
San Francisco City Center – 685 Ellis St. *415-474-5721.*
San Francisco Downtown – 312 Mason St. *415-788-5604.*
San Francisco-Fisherman's Wharf – Upper Fort Mason, Bldg. 240. *415-771-7277.*

MUST KNOW

Hotel and motel chains in San Francsico		
Property	**✆ Contact**	**Web site**
Best Western	800-780-7234	www.bestwestern.com
Comfort, Clarion & Quality Inns	877-424-6423	www.choicehotels.com
Crowne Plaza	800-227-6963	www.crowneplaza.com
Days Inn	800-441-1618	www.daysinn.com
Hilton	800-445-8667	www.hilton.com
Holiday Inn	888-465-4329	www.holiday-inn.com
Howard Johnson	888-637-4861	www.hojo.com
Hyatt	800-323-7249	www.hyatt.com
ITT Sheraton	800-325-3535	www.sheraton.com
Marriott	888-236-2427	www.marriott.com
Omni	800-843-6664	www.omnihotels.com
Radisson	800-967-9033	www.radisson.com
Ramada	888-288-4982	www.ramada.com
Ritz-Carlton	800-542-8680	www.ritzcarlton.com
Westin	800-937-8461	www.westin.com

SPECTATOR SPORTS

San Francisco is a great place to be a spectator where sports are concerned. The city's major professional sports teams include:

Spectator Sports		
Sport/Team	**Venue**	**✆ Phone/Website**
San Francisco Giants		
Baseball Apr–Oct **(NL)**	AT&T Park	Tickets/Info: 415-972-2000 sanfrancisco.giants.mlb.com
Oakland Athletics		
Baseball Apr–Oct **(AL)**	Oakland-Alameda County Coliseum	Tickets/Info: 510-864-5000 oakland.athletics.mlb.com
San Francisco 49ers		
Football Sept–Dec **(NFL)**	Candlestick Park	Tickets/Info: 415-464-9377 www.49ers.com
Oakland Raiders		
Football Sept–Dec **(NFL)**	Oakland-Alameda County Coliseum	Tickets/Info: 510-864-5000 www.raiders.com
Golden State Warriors		
Basketball Nov–Apr **(NBA)**	The Arena at Oakland	Tickets/Info: 510-986-2200 www.nba.com/warriors.com

SAN FRANCISCO

Outsiders have been known to call San Franciscans smug. Why do so many of them walk around smiling? Is it the air? The food? The yoga studios? Ask any of them, and they'll be happy to tell you: they live in the best, most beautiful city in the world.

Mission Dolores

Rick Gerharter/SFCVB

For more than two centuries, European explorers traveling by ship sailed right by the "**Golden Gate**," as the narrow, fog-cloaked entrance of San Francisco Bay came to be called. This entrance was discovered in 1769 by an overland scouting party from Mexico, which was then under Spanish rule. More Spaniards soon arrived, building a small fort called the Presidio and a Catholic missionary outpost, **Mission Dolores** (*see Historic Sites*). The Spanish mandate was to colonize the land and pacify the natives, but the soil was poor for agriculture and the natives proved reluctant converts.

Thousands fled or died of European diseases; others retaliated and were killed. By the time Mexico won its independence from Spain in 1821 and gave the natives land of their own, it was too late. Demoralized, the tribes surrendered their shares to the powerful ranching families known as the Californios.

Noe. De Haro. Bernal. Vallejo. Many streets, neighborhoods and towns in the Bay Area were named after the rancheros, who prospered for about 25 years.

Gradually a scrappy village— **Yerba Buena** (Spanish for "good herb")—took root on the tip of the San Francisco Peninsula. California became part of the United States in 1846, and in 1847 Yerba Buena's name was changed to San Francisco.

"What is this mysterious amalgam that keeps on working?... It is almost in the realm of the metaphysical: a brew of gold rushes and silver bonanzas, sailing ships and shrouded dawns, overnight fortunes and brilliant disasters, bootleg gin, champagne suppers, minestrone and Peking Duck, new-old, beautiful-ugly— a city like no other.... San Francisco lives!" – **Herb Caen, 1967**

In 1848 gold was discovered at Sutter's Mill near Sacramento, and by 1849, some 90,000 hungry prospectors—called "forty-niners"—descended on the city. It was a rambunctious time. Brothels, flophouses, gambling halls, and opium dens were rife, as were, perhaps surprisingly, opera houses and theaters. Natural disaster struck on the morning of April 18, 1906, in the form of a massive earthquake on the San Andreas Fault. By noon, 52 fires were burning throughout the city, eventually devouring 514 blocks and leaving 250,000 people homeless. Yet a plucky sprit prevailed in the refugee camps. The smoke had barely cleared when rebuilding began. Over the next 50 years San Francisco took on its contemporary character. In the 1920s and 1930s, its progressivism came to the fore, as unions won major gains for workers, despite the Great Depression.

Later the city opened its arms to mainstream society's outcasts—from the disaffected beat poets of the 1950s to idealistic flower children of the 1960s. Gay liberation and feminism, which took hold in the 1970s, are still powerful forces today.

Not that the city doesn't wear a suit once in a while. As computer companies flourished, city coffers bulged. In the late 1990s, hundreds of Internet start-ups set up shop in warehouses **South of Market**. The bubble burst in 2000, leaving nearly half of those offices vacant, but San Franciscans held their ground. In 2004 housing prices remained at an all-time high and the economy was rebounding. Ups and downs are as much a part of the urban fabric as those outlandish hills. Like tourists thronging its cable cars, San Franciscans just hang on and enjoy the ride.

Fast Facts

- **Area:** 49 square miles
- **Population:** 790,000
- **Visitors:** 16 million annually
- **Number-one reason for visiting:** Atmosphere and ambience
- **Number of high rises (eight or more stories):** 501
- **Number of Victorian houses:** 14,000
- **Official Motto:** "Gold in peace, iron in war"

View toward Financial District from North Beach, San Francisco

©Daniella Nowitz/Apa Publications

NEIGHBORHOODS

Just as San Francisco has microclimates—patches of sun and fog—it also has what could be called microcultures. These are its neighborhoods. Each has its own character, a special quality that is generated, not surprisingly, by the people who live there. So spend some time strolling the city streets and be transported into these fascinating self-sustaining worlds.

Chinatown★★★

Roughly bounded by Bush, Stockton & Kearny Sts., and Columbus Ave. & Broadway. www.sanfranciscochinatown.com.

Teeming Chinatown spills down the eastern slope of Nob Hill, bridging the Financial District and North Beach. Within its 24 compact blocks you'll find a whole world. Streets and alleyways are lined with savory restaurants and dim sum "palaces," tea shops, vegetable markets, jewelry stores and temples.

The district got its start around 1849, when thousands of Cantonese treasure seekers crossed the Pacific and ventured up toward Sutter's Mill in search of gold. By the 1860s, Chinatown was well established. Bound by culture and language, residents also stuck together for safety. During the economic depressions of the 1870s, riotous bands of unemployed Anglos periodically stormed Chinatown, beating and sometimes killing men who, they felt, stole their jobs by working for lower wages. The Chinese Exclusion Act of 1882 effectively barred thousands of Chinese laborers (though not merchants) from bringing their families to the States. As a result, Chinatown was predominantly male well into the 20C. Opium dens, brothels and gambling halls proliferated, and turf wars regularly broke out among the "tongs," or local gangs, to control profits.

Conditions improved after the Exclusion Act was repealed in 1943 and more legitimate businesses took hold. Today the neighborhood, one of the most densely populated in the country with some 13,716 residents, remains a tight-knit community that fiercely protects its Asian heritage.

The Streets of Chinatown

Grant Avenue★★ – *See Shopping.* Chinatown's Main Street, the eight blocks of Grant Avenue between Bush Street and Broadway, abound in architectural chinoiserie: brightly painted balconies, curved tile

Chinatown

Brigitta L. House/MICHELIN

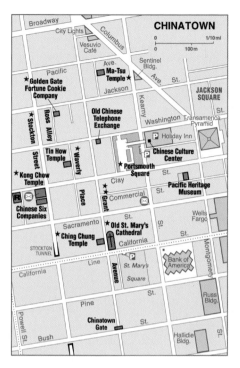

CHINATOWN

Broadway
City Lights
Columbus
Vesuvio Café
Ma-Tsu Temple ★
Sentinel Bldg.
Pacific Ave.
★ Golden Gate Fortune Cookie Company
Jackson
JACKSON SQUARE
Ross Alley
Stockton
Old Chinese Telephone Exchange
Kearny
Washington
Transamerica Pyramid
Holiday Inn
Tin How Temple
Waverly
★ Chinese Culture Center
Portsmouth Square
★ Kong Chow Temple
Place
Clay
Grant
Pacific Heritage Museum
Commercial St.
Chinese Six Companies
Sacramento
St.
Wells Fargo
★ Old St. Mary's Cathedral
★ Ching Chung Temple
California
STOCKTON TUNNEL
Montgomery
California
Line
Avenue
St. Mary's Square
Bank of America
Pine
Russ Bldg.
Powell St.
Chinatown Gate
Bush
St.
Hallidie Bldg.

rooflines, and staggered towers. The ceramic carp and dragons on the roof of the Chinatown Gate (*Grant Ave. at Bush St.*) represent good luck.

Portsmouth Square★ – *Bounded by Clay, Kearny & Washington Sts.* Chinatown centers on Portsmouth Square, a small park where

residents practice t'ai chi in the mornings and socialize into the night. It was here in 1846 that Captain John Montgomery officially claimed the city, then called Yerba Buena, for the US.

Stockton Street★ – Shoppers throng the produce, fresh fish and poultry markets flanking the four

Chinese New Year Parade

Crowds fill the streets and the sound of thousands of popping firecrackers fills the night air each year (date varies from late Jan–late Feb) as the Chinese New Year Parade makes its raucous way through downtown. The largest celebration of its kind outside China, San Francisco's Chinatown event rings in the lunar new year with brightly costumed stilt walkers, acrobats, lion dancers and the grand finale—the 200ft-long Golden Dragon, decorated with colored lights and carried by a cadre of 100 people. For information, check online at *www.onlyinsanfrancisco.org* or *www.sanfranciscochinatown.com.*

NEIGHBORHOODS

blocks between Clay Street and Broadway.

Waverly Place★ – *Off Washington St. between Grant Ave. & Stockton St.* This two-block alley is one of Chinatown's most colorful. Balconies are painted in symbolic hues: red for happiness, green for longevity, black for money, and yellow for luck.

Chinese Historical Society of America Museum – [R] *See map. 965 Clay St. 415-391-1188. www.chsa.org. Tue–Fri 12–5pm Sat 11am–4pm (Closed Sunday, Monday, and Holidays).*
The society's exhibits explore the role of Chinese immigrants in the Western world in both the past and present.

Financial District★★

The Financial District is very much a place of business, and its character changes completely at different times of day. Traffic, pedestrians and bicycle messengers clog the streets during morning and evening rush hours *(7am–9am & 4pm–6pm)*. Take-out sandwich shops and salad bars do a brisk

Tadich Grill

240 California St. 415-391-1849. www.tadichgrill.com Closed Sun. Fresh fish is the fare, bulls and bears the topic of choice at this San Francisco institution, which began life as a coffee stand during the Gold Rush. Go for the sole, sand dabs, seafood salads, and for the no-nonsense service by white-jacketed waiters.

business at lunch. But at night the area is practically deserted—plan accordingly.

Despite its modern appearance, the Financial District harbors some of the city's earliest history. It was here, along what was then a sheltered cove, that the village of Yerba Buena grew up in the 1840s. At the outbreak of the Mexican-American War in 1846, US troops took control of the town from the Spanish-speaking Californios and renamed it San Francisco. Until 1848 there were fewer than 500 residents. Then came the Gold Rush of 1849. Within months, some 90,000 treasure-hungry transients had converged on the settlement, some opening businesses to serve the exploding population. A city was born.

Half of what we think of as the Financial District didn't even exist then. Present-day Montgomery Street was a muddy path along the shoreline of the bay. But because nearly everyone at that time came by boat, there was a huge need for piers. Jutting out from the shore, the piers got longer and longer, essentially becoming roads. Soon the space between was filled in with the remains of Rincon Hill, an inconvenient protuberance south

Financial District

Brigitta L. House/MICHELIN

of Market. Hundreds of abandoned ships were buried.

The 1906 earthquake and fire destroyed the district, but it was largely rebuilt by 1909. Many of the new buildings were done in the Classical style; then in the 1920s the first skyscrapers started going up. By the 1970s, after the Transamerica Pyramid was erected, preservationists were starting to panic and strict limitations were placed on the height and bulk of new buildings. Since then most new construction has happened South of Market (*see p 34*).

Financial District Highlights

555 California★★ –
555 California St. Formerly the Bank of America Center, this 52-story, dark-red behemoth (1971, Skidmore, Owings and Merrill) competes with the Transamerica Pyramid for dominance of the skyline.

Bank of California★★ –
400 California St. Now the Union Bank of California, this exquisite, classically proportioned bank (1907, Bliss and Faville) displays the energy and resources put into rebuilding the city after the 1906 fire. A regal, coffered ceiling tops the banking hall.

345 California Center★★ –
3*45 California St.* Two angular towers linked by a glass-enclosed "sky bridge" cap this futuristic skyscraper, designed in 1987 by the prestigious firm of Skidmore, Owings and Merrill.

Hallidie Building★★ – *130-150 Sutter St.* One of San Francisco's most noteworthy works of architecture, the seven-story office block was designed by Willis Polk, completed in 1917, and named

after Andrew Hallidie, inventor of the cable car. Because the façade is formed by a modular grid of glass panes hanging from a reinforced concrete frame, the building is considered the world's first glass-curtain-walled structure.

Jackson Square★★ – *Bounded by Washington, Montgomery & Sansome Sts. and Pacific Ave. See Landmarks.*

🏨 **Palace Hotel★★** – *2 New Montgomery St. 415-392-8600. www.luxuryresortcollection.com/palacehotel.* Constructed in 1875 by financier William Ralston, the Palace gained a reputation as the most opulent hotel in the West until it was gutted in the 1906 fire. The Palace reopened in 1909, and today the **Garden Court★★**, with its leaded-glass canopy is the hotel's most luxurious public space.

Palace Hotel

Palace Hotel

Belden Place

A piece of Old World Europe transplanted to San Francisco, this one-block-long alley extends from Pine to Bush Street just east of Kearny Street. It is lined with exquisite cafes serving international fare—French (Plouf and Cafe Bastille), Catalan (B44), and Mediterranean (Taverna), just to name a few.

NEIGHBORHOODS

25

Transamerica Pyramid★★ – *600 Montgomery St. See Landmarks.*
Union Square★★ – At the Financial District's western edge is Union Square, a formal park named on the eve of the Civil War, when it hosted numerous rallies in support of the Union. Spiffed up with a new granite plaza in 2002, the square now forms the centerpiece of a posh retail district (*see Shopping*).

Nob Hill★★

The upscale residential district lodged between Pacific Heights and Chinatown, Nob Hill got its name for the titans of industry who once lived here—"nob" is a contraction of "nabob," a term for European adventurers who made huge fortunes in India and the East. These nabobs came in two waves. The first were the "Big Four" railroad magnates, Leland Stanford, Charles Crocker, Mark Hopkins and Collis Huntington. Formerly middle-class Sacramento merchants, these newly minted millionaires built sprawling mansions atop Nob Hill in the 1870s. In the 1880s they were joined by two of the four

Hobnob Tours

To get a thorough grounding in **Nob Hill** history, take the HobNob walking tour, which departs weekdays from the Fairmont Hotel *(2 hrs; 10am & 1:30pm; 650-814-6303; www.hobnobtours.com).*

"Bonanza Kings," James Fair and James Flood, who profited mightily off Nevada's Comstock silver lode. Engineer Andrew Hallidie's "folly," the cable car, brought more development to the 376ft summit after the establishment of the California (1878) and Powell Street (1888) lines.

The only structure to withstand the 1906 earthquake and fire was Flood's 1885 brownstone mansion, now the exclusive **Pacific-Union Club** *(1000 California St.)*. Today one of the **best views**★★★ in the city can be had from the Top of the Mark bar in the InterContinental Mark Hopkins hotel (*see Nightlife*).
Cable Car Museum★★ – *1201 Mason St. at Washington St. See Museums.*

The Fairmont San Francisco

The Fairmont San Francisco

MUST SEE

View of North Beach area with Saints Peter and Paul Church and Coit Tower

©Can Balcioglu/iStockphoto.com

🏨 Fairmont Hotel★★
Main entrance on Mason St.
between California & Sacramento Sts
415-772-5000. www.fairmont.com.
See Hotels.

In one of her first big commissions, architect Julia Morgan oversaw the restoration of this Italian Renaissance hotel, which was nearly complete when the 1906 earthquake struck. On April 18, 1907, exactly one year later, the Fairmont reopened. The ornate main lobby, with its massive marble pillars and wrought-iron balconies, is worth a peek, as is the supremely kitschy Tonga Room (*see Nightlife*).

Grace Cathedral★
1051 Taylor St. at California St.
415-749-6300.
www.gracecathedral.org.

The third-largest Episcopal cathedral in the US, completed in 1964, anchors the crest of Nob Hill, its French Gothic spires soaring majestically over the city. The bronze **Gates of Paradise★** in the eastern portal are the cathedral's most prized architectural feature; at 16ft high, they are divided into 10 richly ornamented panels depicting scenes from the Old Testament.

North Beach★★

One of the sunniest and liveliest neighborhoods in the city gets its character from the Italians who came to dominate the area around 1900. Though they're no longer in the majority residentially, the dozens of cafés, restaurants, delicatessens and bars here attest to their interpretation of "the good life." A ragtag assortment of beret-wearing poets and artists who called themselves the "beat generation" shared this view from the mid-1950s to the mid-1960s. They were driven out by the busloads of tourists who came through to see what all the fuss was about. Many Italian shopkeepers remained. Columbus Avenue, the neighborhood's main thoroughfare, cuts diagonally from the Transamerica Pyramid to the Cannery on Fisherman's Wharf (*see Landmarks*). It's packed with places to eat, drink and be entertained (*see Restaurants and Nightlife*).

Coit Tower★★★ – *Atop*
Telegraph Hill. See Landmarks.
City Lights Bookstore★ –
261 Columbus Ave. See Shopping.
Beatnik Lawrence Ferlinghetti's book nook.

Filbert Steps★★

If you're visiting Coit Tower on foot, be sure to take this steep, celebrated pathway down the east flank of Telegraph Hill. Views look out onto treehouse-like cottages and their well-tended gardens. The Streamline Moderne apartment house at 1360 Montgomery appeared in the 1947 Bogart-Bacall film *Dark Passage*.

Saints Peter and Paul Church★
666 Filbert St. 415-421-0809.
Overlooking **Washington Square★**, North Beach's premier picnic park, the twin-spired church is fondly known as the Italian cathedral. Baseball great Joe DiMaggio, who grew up in the neighborhood, and screen legend Marilyn Monroe had wedding pictures taken in front of the church—but contrary to local lore, the two weren't married here (the actual ceremony took place at City Hall). Step inside to see the spectacular 40ft-high altar, featuring a sculptural reproduction of Da Vinci's Last Supper.

Pacific Heights★★

Great for an afternoon stroll, this tony residential neighborhood holds some of the city's finest (and biggest) houses and loveliest views. The district stretches across a high, east-west ridge between Van Ness Avenue and the Presidio. After the 1906 quake and fire, many wealthy San Franciscans who had lost homes on Nob Hill resettled in Pacific Heights, where the parcels were bigger. Most of the district's mansions date from this period. Yet thanks to the neighborhood's distance from the downtown inferno, many "gingerbread"

Haas-Lilienthal House

Anne Marie Scott/MICHELIN

Victorians remain from the 1880s and 1890s. These were built for well-to-do families but were actually the "prefab" houses of the era: fish-scale shingles, ogive-shaped windows, and finely carved verge boards could be bought directly from lumber mills and added to the design.
When you visit, bear in mind that streets ascend and descend abruptly, sometimes as much as 100ft in one block. For an in-depth look at the neighborhood, consider taking the two-hour Pacific Heights **Walking Tour** offered by San Francisco Architectural Heritage *(Sun 12:30pm; for details, call Haas-Lilienthal House)*.

Haas-Lilienthal House★★
2007 Franklin St. 415-441-3000. www.sfheritage.org. Visit by guided tour only, Wed & Sat noon–3pm, Sun 11am–4pm. Closed major holidays. $8.
San Francisco's only fully furnished Queen Anne Victorian open to the public, this imposing gray edifice was built in 1886 for William Haas, a prominent wholesaler. It has patterned siding, ornately

bracketed gables, and a deceptive corner tower with windows 10ft above the floor. Within, two parlors, a dining room, and one of the original six bedrooms reflect the period from the 1880s to the 1920s in their decor.

Spreckels Mansion★★
2080 Washington St. Not open to the public. Of all the many grand mansions in Pacific Heights, none is more ostentatious than the French Baroque-style palace built in 1913 for sugar magnate Adolph Spreckels and his wife. Best-selling author Danielle Steel now lives here.

Marina

The Marina and Cow Hollow
In the mid-19C the sloped valley between Russian Hill and the hills of the Presidio was a grassland of dairy farms, popularly known as Cow Hollow. After the 1906 earthquake, the shallow flats off the shore of Cow Hollow were extended with landfill to create new land for the buildings of the 1915 Panama International Exposition. When the fair closed, those buildings on the northern waterfront were demolished—

except for the **Palace of Fine Arts** (*see Landmarks*) and replaced with a middle-class residential housing area that became known as the Marina District.

Disaster struck with the 1989 Loma Prieta earthquake, when the landfill beneath some buildings liquefied, causing them to collapse. The neighborhood survived, however, and remains one of the city's most desirable residential neighborhoods, especially among young professionals who enjoy the plethora of trendy boutiques, upscale restaurants and cafés, and lively nightlife scene that fill **Union** and **Chestnut streets** (*See Shopping*).

Fort Mason Center
(*See Historic Sites*)
415-345-7400. fortmason.org.
This bayside complex of barracks, warehouses and docks was the embarkation point for the Pacific in World War II. A leading example of adaptive reuse, the former fort now houses non-profit and cultural organizations, theatres, museums (*See Museums*), and the head-quarters of the Golden Gate National Recreation Area (*See Parks*).

Caffeine and Conversation
Besides making perfect cappuccinos, these bustling cafes offer a glimpse into the daily life of North Beach. Most are open from morning until midnight (or at least 10:30pm) and serve, in addition to coffee, wine and beer, pastries (cannoli!) and sandwiches.

Caffè Trieste – *601 Vallejo St. 415-392-6739.*
Mario's Bohemian Cigar Store – *566 Columbus Ave. 415-362-0536.*
Caffè Puccini – *411 Columbus Ave. 415-989-7033.*
Caffè Greco – *423 Columbus Ave. 415-397-6261.*
Tosca Cafe – *242 Columbus Ave. 415-986-9651. Open daily 5pm–2am.*
A great place for a late-night cocktail, this 1940s-style bar plays opera, Big Band jazz, and Sinatra on its jukebox.

NEIGHBORHOODS

Shopping in Pacific Heights

Fillmore Street between Bush and Jackson streets is Pacific Heights' retail corridor. It's surprisingly unpretentious, with a browser-friendly blend of book shops and boutiques, as well as numerous cafés.

For a good strong jolt of coffee, try **Peet's** *(2197 Fillmore St.; 415-563-9930)*. Nearby **Cow Hollow** also has some interesting shopping, along Union Street. *See Must Shop.*

Exploratorium

3601 Lyon St. Tue–Sun 10am–5pm. Closed major holidays. Adults $15, ages 13–17 $12, ages 4–12 $10. 415-561-0360. www.exploratorium.edu.
Located in the annex structure of the Palace of Fine Arts, this innovative and highly interactive museum of science, art, and human perception boasts more than 650 exhibits organized around the areas of sound, vision and the life sciences. In 2013, the Exploratorium will be moving to Pier 15.

Civic Center★

Bounded by Market St., Van Ness Ave. & Golden Gate Ave.

San Francisco's "town center," as it were, has one life during the day, when government offices are in full swing, and another at night, when concert goers flock to performances in its theaters. The Beaux-Arts buildings here are considered to be one of the finest groups of this style in the US. Well into the 19C, city government occupied a variety of buildings

girdling Portsmouth Square in present-day Chinatown. But in 1872 it was decided that something grander was in order. Finally, in 1905, architects Daniel Burnham of Chicago and Willis Polk, a local, presented what was called "the Burnham Plan," featuring grand monuments, wide boulevards, and other City Beautiful hallmarks to remake San Francisco along the lines of Paris or Washington, DC. After the 1906 catastrophe, however, most people simply rebuilt on the old street grid. Civic Center, a small-scale version of the plan, comes courtesy of the government that commissioned it. In 1945 the area played a significant role in world history. From April to June, 1945, the United Nations convened in the War Memorial Opera House, and the UN Charter was signed in the Herbst Theatre.

Asian Art Museum★★★ – *200 Larkin St. See Museums.*
City Hall★★ – *Entrance on Polk St., between McAllister & Grove Sts. See Landmarks.*

San Francisco War Memorial and Performing Arts Center★★
401 Van Ness Ave. 415-552-8338. sfwmpac.org Visit by guided tour only, Mon 10am–2pm (except holidays); $5. Student and seniors admissions $3. See Performing Arts.
Three exceptional buildings contain the city's most renowned performing-arts institutions, two of which saw the founding of the UN in 1945. On the north end is the **Veterans Building [F]** (see map on inside front cover) home to the (relatively intimate) 916-seat Herbst Theatre. The UN Charter was signed here. South of the

San Francisco Opera's War Memorial Opera House

San Francisco Opera

Veterans Building is an attractive formal courtyard designed by Thomas Church.

The complex's centerpiece, the 1932 **War Memorial Opera House** [**E**] (*see map on inside front cover*), was the first city-owned opera house in the US. The San Francisco Opera and Ballet perform in its 3146-seat auditorium, which is distinguished by a 27ft star chandelier and a gold brocatelle proscenium curtain that weighs one ton. From April to June 1945, the Conference on International Organization met here to establish the UN's bylaws.

To the south stands the strikingly modern **Louise M. Davies Symphony Hall** (1980). Though some critics found its curving glass facade out of sync with the Beaux-Arts aesthetic of the area, it has proved a festive place to see a concert, and particularly appropriate to the challenging new repertoire championed by conductor Michael Tilson Thomas (*see Performing Arts*).

San Francisco Public Library★
100 Larkin St. 415-557-4400. http://sfpl.org.

Opened in 1996, the city's new library turns a contemporary eye on Beaux-Arts classicism. The gleaming exterior is sheathed in granite from the same quarry that provided stone for the City Hall and War Memorial. The seven-story interior is decked out with catwalk bridges, artworks,

Dashiell Hammett Tour

Tours leave at noon from the northwest corner of the Main Library at 100 Larkin St. May–June and by appointment. 510-287-9540. www.donherron.com. Foggy nights, deserted street corners, a fedora dipped below one eye, a trench coat with the collar up. Ever since John Huston shot *The Maltese Falcon* here, the city has become synonymous with mystery and intrigue. See the seedy bars and tawdry hotels so beloved by novelist Dashiell Hammett, who worked in San Francisco as a Pinkerton detective before creating his alter ego, Sam Spade. Don Herron knows his stuff: he's been leading these celebrated walks for 25 years.

NEIGHBORHOODS

computers, and an asymmetrical skylit atrium. Changing displays of art and literature are presented in the lower-level Jewett Exhibition Gallery.

Hayes Valley

Just a few blocks west of Civic Center, artsy Hayes Valley is a great place to eat and shop (*see Shopping*) if you're in the area, with a number of upscale clothing and furniture boutiques, several art galleries, and a dozen acclaimed restaurants serving everything from sushi to schnitzel.

Keep in mind that most eateries require reservations on evenings with symphony and opera performances at the San Francisco War Memorial Performing Arts Center.

Haight-Ashbury★

Centered on Haight St. between Central Ave. & Stanyan St.

Although more than three decades have passed since the Human Be-In and the Summer of Love, a countercultural ethos still clings to the Haight, particularly on Haight Street itself. The stretch between Central and Stanyan streets, known to locals as the "Upper Haight," is packed with thrift stores, boutiques, and coffeehouses (*see Shopping*).

Ambitious fixer-uppers have made their homes here too, drawn by the tremendous concentration of Victorian homes—90 percent of the housing stock predates 1922. Stroll along Page, Masonic and Waller streets to see lovely examples of the fanciful Queen Anne style.

Mission District★

Roughly bounded by 14th, Cesar Chavez, Dolores & Potrero Sts.

This sunny southern neighborhood has a young, funky feel, with artists, hipsters, and activists coexisting with a vibrant Latino community. The Catholic Mission anchored a small village here in the early 1800s, but none of it remains. Instead you'll find shoulder-to-shoulder Italianate row houses, some dating to the 1870s.
Mission Dolores★ – *16th & Dolores Sts. See Historic Sites.*

Haight-Ashbury

MUST SEE

Maestrapiece

Brigitta L. House/MICHELIN

Maestrapiece
***Women's Building, 3543 18th St.
at Lapidge St.*** Covering two
exterior walls, this is one of the
Mission's newest, biggest and most
colorful murals, a celebration of
the area's rich Latino and feminist
heritage. Look for Georgia O'Keeffe,
Audre Lorde and Rigoberta
Menchú in the design.

Valencia Street – *See Shopping.*

Russian Hill★

***Bounded by Francisco, Taylor,
Pacific & Polk Sts.***

Along with neighbors Nob Hill
and Telegraph Hill, Russian Hill
offers some of the best vistas in
the city, along with a glimpse
of its largely forgotten literary
history. As the story goes, the hill
was named in the mid-19C when
the graves of Russian seal hunters
were discovered atop the crest of

present-day Vallejo Street. But it
wasn't until the 1880s, when the
cable car provided easy access to
its summit, that people actually
started moving here en masse.
The Powell-Hyde and Powell-
Mason lines are still the best means
to get to the top.
Literary Legacy – From 1856
through the 1890s, Catherine
Atkinson's home at 1032 Broadway
served as a salon for Mark Twain,
Ambrose Bierce, Robert Louis
Stevenson, and other big-name
writers. Ina Coolbrith convened
a similar group at her house at
1604 Taylor Street. Beat writer Jack
Kerouac spent six months on the
hill in 1952; he stayed with friends
at 29 Russell Street and worked on
several novels, including *On the
Road.* Nearby Macondray Lane
also served as a model for Barbary
Lane in Armistead Maupin's *Tales
of the City.* Evidently the hill is an
inspiring place.
Lombard Street★★★ –
See Landmarks.
Views★★ – The Taylor Street summit
of the Vallejo Street Stairway—the
centerpiece of Ina Coolbrith Park—
offers magnificent eastward-facing

Zazie

*941 Cole St. 415-564-5332.
www.zaziesf.com.* An ideal
beginning or ending to a day
spent exploring Haight-Ashbury
and Golden Gate Park, this tiny
Provençal bistro (named after
Louis Malle's film of the same
name) is a local favorite for
breakfast, lunch and dinner.
Enjoy Belgian waffles with
caramelized pecans, salade
Niçoise, and an assortment of
savory stews and sandwiches.

Castro District

Castro District

Bounded roughly by 16th to 22nd Sts. and Douglass to Dolores Sts. Epicenter of gay San Francisco, "the Castro," as it's called, hums with energy night and day. In the 1950s, enterprising gay designers began purchasing the Castro's 19C Victorians at rock-bottom prices and fixing them up. Though prices are significantly higher, the trend continues today.

The action's at **Castro Street** (between Market & 20th Sts.), a thrumming corridor of shops and bars, and home to the **Castro Theatre★** movie palace (see Nightlife). **Market Street** (between Castro & Church Sts.) and **Church Street** (between Market & 17th Sts.) offer a fun mix of shops and restaurants that appeal to folks of all persuasions.

views of the bay. At the corner of Jones and Green streets, views extend north over Alcatraz.
San Francisco Art Institute★ – *800 Chestnut St. See Museums.*

South of Market★

Roughly bounded by 12th, Market & King Sts. and the Embarcadero.

San Francisco's hardscrabble history meets its high-tech future in the large, heterogeneous region known as South of Market, or SoMa. In 1847 city planner Jasper O'Farrell gave SoMa its distinctive look, making its streets twice as wide and its blocks four times as large as those north of market, and setting the whole area at a 45-degree angle to the grid. The idea was to make room for industry, and it worked. Foundries, gasworks, shipyards, refineries and breweries took hold here. As manufacturing declined in the mid-20C, architects, graphic designers, software companies, and publishers divvied up former industrial buildings and warehouses into loftlike offices. Other large spaces have been converted to restaurants, clubs and galleries (see Nightlife) or retail stores (see Shopping) in this up-and-coming area.

Town Hall

342 Howard St. 415-908-3900. www.townhallsf.com. Hearty regional American fare rules the roost at this new restaurant, three blocks east of Yerba Buena Gardens. Occupying a beautifully renovated 1907 warehouse, Town Hall suggests an Adirondack eating hall with its exposed brick walls and white wainscoting. If you want to make a new friend, grab a seat at the 14ft-long communal table by the bar and order the irresistible butterscotch and chocolate pot de crème.

San Francisco Museum of Modern Art★★ – *151 Third St. See Museums.*

AT&T Park★★ – *Third & Kings Sts., at the Embarcadero. See For Fun.*

Yerba Buena Gardens★★ *Mission St. between Third & Fourth Sts. www.yerbabuena.org.* This family-friendly complex of parks and museums, galleries and theaters has quickly established itself as one of the city's most vital entertainment hubs. It centers on the rolling green Esplanade, a lawn used for picnics and outdoor concerts. A waterfall monument to Dr. Martin Luther King, Jr. provides an appropriate backdrop.

Yerba Buena Center for the Arts★ **[K]** *(see map on inside front cover; Third & Mission Sts.; 415-978-2787; www.yerba buenaarts.org)* hosts thought provoking art exhibits that change regularly. The building also contains a 750-seat theater *(see Performing Arts).*

Metreon★, Rooftop at Yerba Buena Gardens★★ and **Zeum★** – *At Yerba Buena Gardens. See For Kids.*

Contemporary Jewish Museum – *736 Mission Street. See Museums.*

Zeum

Tom Bross/SFCVB

NEIGHBORHOODS

LANDMARKS

In most cities, landmarks are things that people build to add distinction. San Francisco, by contrast, had distinction before anything was built. Its undulating hills, expansive bay and dramatic fog all make it, in the words of Robert Redford, "the most beautiful place in the world." The following landmarks offer angles, both historical and cinematic, from which to appreciate it.

Alcatraz★★★

Access by ferry only (see sidebar below). 415-705-5555. www.nps.gov/alcatraz. Open daily May–Sept 9:30am–6:30pm. Rest of the year daily 9:30am–4:30pm. Closed Jan 1, Dec 25 & Thanksgiving. Ferry fee includes admission to island.

So close, and yet so far. Prisoners at "the Rock" had a tantalizing view of San Francisco, but the mile-and-a-half span between the two landmasses was virtually unbridgeable. Would-be escapees drowned or froze—if they weren't shot or captured first—and there was scant traffic in the other direction. The first inmates came to Alcatraz in the 1850s, when a military fortress was established here by President Millard Fillmore. The military transferred jurisdiction

Escape to Alcatraz

Alcatraz Cruises is the only line that offers service to Alcatraz. *Ferries depart from Pier 41 on Fisherman's Wharf May–Sept daily 9:30am–6:30pm. Rest of the year until 4:20pm. 415-981-7625. http://www.alcatrazcruises.com. $26 adults; $33 for night tour.* The 15-minute ferry trip offers sensational views of the city, the island, and the Golden Gate Bridge. Reservations should be made at least a week in advance. Dress warmly and prepare to stay about two and a half hours.

to the US Department of Justice in 1933. For the next 30 years, the penitentiary was home to the most "desperate and irredeemable criminals" in the US, including Al "Scarface" Capone, Machine Gun Kelly, and Robert "Birdman" Stroud.

Alcatraz

P. Fuszard/SFCVB

Telegraph Hill and Coit Tower

Lewis Sommer/SFCVB

The conditions were unimaginably brutal, with one guard to every three prisoners, a strict no-talking policy, and "dark holes" of solitary confinement for rule breakers. Despite the odds of survival, 36 men tried to escape; it's still not clear if the most famous attempt, made by three men in 1962, was successful. Their bodies were never found. Alcatraz was designated part of the Golden Gate National Recreation Area in 1972. Tours of the ruins have been fascinating visitors ever since. Don't miss the bleak **concrete cellhouse★★**, built by convicts in 1911.

Coit Tower★★★

Summit of Telegraph Hill. 415-362-0808. Mar–Sept daily 10am-5:30pm. Oct–Feb daily 9am–4:30pm. Closed Thanksgiving Day, Christmas Day and New Year's Eve. To avoid the steep climb, take the 39-Coit bus from Washington Square in North Beach.

Though less than a third of the height of the Transamerica Pyramid, this svelte 180ft column rivals that giant skyscraper as the city's best-known landmark. Why? In part because it's boosted into the clouds by 274ft **Telegraph Hill★**. But Coit Tower is also a monument to one resident's pride in her hometown.

As the story goes, when Lillie Hitchcock Coit (1843–1929) was a little girl in San Francisco, a firefighter rescued her from a burning building. Later, when she was 15, she came upon Knickerbocker Engine Company No. 5 struggling up Telegraph Hill en route to a blaze. Throwing down her schoolbooks, she rallied onlookers to help the firemen. To show their gratitude, they made her their mascot.

Coit remembered the incident for the rest of her life. In her will she left $125,000 to the city of San Francisco, the bulk of which went toward the construction of this tower, designed by Arthur Brown, Jr., and completed in 1934. (It was not meant to look like a firehose nozzle, as some locals persist in saying.)

Views★★★ – The top of the tower, reached via elevator and stairs, affords the best views in a city that, as Alfred Hitchcock said, doesn't have a bad angle. If you're afraid of heights, Pioneer Park at the base of the tower also has **spectacular views★★★**.

LANDMARKS

Murals★★ – In 1934, at the depth of the Great Depression, 26 out-of-work painters and their assistants were commissioned to create 19 fresco murals in the lobby of newly constructed Coit Tower. The theme, "contemporary life in California," was given a radical twist by the artists, who strongly identified with the thousands left penniless, homeless, or unemployed by the stock market crash. Several of the painters clearly advocated revolution, which was a real possibility in a year that a general strike shut down the city for four days. Luckily, a movement to destroy the murals was voted down and the lobby was opened to the public in October 1934 to great acclaim.

Fisherman's Wharf★★★

Along Jefferson St. and the Embarcadero between Van Ness & Stockton Sts. www.fishermanswharf.org.

Locals may avoid it like the plague, but this mile-long stretch of waterfront at the city's northern tip has blossomed over the past 50 years into San Francisco's most popular tourist attraction. Six piers jut out into the bay, offering everything from carousel rides and discount

Fisherman's Wharf sign

Brigita L. House/MICHELIN

shopping (Pier 39) to maritime history (Hyde Street Pier). Nearby you'll find slips for the ferries to Alcatraz and Marin County. This is not the city's original shoreline. Shortly after the Gold Rush, Henry "Honest Harry" Meiggs—councilman, entrepreneur, and later the most notorious embezzler of funds in the city's early history—constructed a wharf extending 1,600ft from present-day Francisco and Powell streets across North Point Cove into the bay. In the 1860s the cove (present-day North Beach) was filled with rock blasted from the eastern face of Telegraph Hill. A manufacturing and industrial zone grew up along this new flat stretch, which had clear access to the ships

Tips for Visiting Fisherman's Wharf

As with most sites in the city, public transportation is the best way to get to Fisherman's Wharf. Take the Powell-Hyde cable car to its northern terminus if you want to visit the more historical western end of the wharf. The F-Market streetcar will deposit you at the east end, next to **Aquarium of the Bay★**. Jefferson Street is thronged on most weekends throughout the year; try a weekday if you want to avoid at least some of the crowds. For lunch, consider getting a ladle of creamy clam chowder in a hollowed-out loaf of sourdough bread, the wharf's signature dish.

that at the time connected the burgeoning city with the rest of the world. Longshoremen and sailors ruled the roost. And yes, there were fishermen.

From the 1870s onward, most were of Italian descent, and their influence lives on in the restaurants of the area. By the 1950s, the bay had been overfished, forcing fleets out into the ocean, and the shipping industry had moved to Oakland. Tourism, starting with the opening of the National Maritime Museum in 1951, saved the area from decline even as it obscured much of the history it meant to celebrate.

Hyde Street Pier★★
Jefferson St. at Hyde St. 415-561-7100. www.nps.gov/safr/. Open daily 9:30am–5pm, Jun-Aug until 5:30pm.

Once a ferry terminal, the westernmost pier of Fisherman's Wharf now showcases six historic ships, part of San Francisco Maritime National Historical Park. The grandest is the **Balclutha★★**, a three-masted, square-rigger launched in Glasgow, Scotland, in 1886. **The Eureka★**, a sidewheel ferry built in 1890, still ranks as the world's largest floating wooden structure. **The C.A. Thayer★**, an 1895 codfisher, is one of only two three-masted wooden sailing schooners in the US.

The Cannery★★ – *2801 Leavenworth St. See Shopping.*
Ghirardelli Square★★ – *900 North Point St. See Shopping.*
USS Pampanito★★ – *Pier 45. 415-775-1943. www.maritime.org 9am–6pm Sun–Thurs and 9pm–8pm on Fri and Sat and 9pm–7:30pm on Sun .* A terrific self-guided audio tour of this World War II-era submarine captures the claustrophobia, fear and boredom of life underwater.
SS Jeremiah O'Brien★ – *Pier 45. 415-544-0100. www.ssjeremiah obrien.org. Open year-round daily 9am–4pm. Closed Jan 1, Thanksgiving Day & Dec 25.* This lovingly restored 441ft vessel formed part of the 5,000-ship armada that stormed Normandy Beach in 1944. Self-guided tours explore the wheelhouse, crew's quarters and engine room (featured in the film *Titanic*).
National Maritime Museum★ – *Beach St. at Polk St. See Museums.*

Hyde Street Pier

Brigitta L. House/MICHELIN

Playful Pinnipeds

One of San Francisco's modern mysteries is why, in January 1990, a boisterous pod of sea lions took up residence at **Pier 39**. Some say the 1989 Loma Prieta earthquake shook them out of their former digs; others credit the area's proximity to a large herring run. In any case, the original group of 50 told their friends and multiplied.

Today up to 300 playful pinnipeds winter here, and some even stick around in the summer, when most of the pod shoves off for the Channel Islands.

Pier 39★

Beach Street & The Embarcadero. 415-705-5500. www.pier39.com. Check website for hours.

A theme-park atmosphere prevails on this double-decked shopping mall. If you can successfully dodge the crowds, you'll find 93 shops and restaurants, an **aquarium★**, a large-format theater, a carousel, and more (*see For Kids*).

Golden Gate Bridge

Phillip H. Coblentz/SFCVB

Golden Gate Bridge★★★

Hwy. 101 between Marin County and San Francisco. 415-921-5858. www.goldengatebridge.org. Pedestrian access, via the east sidewalk, to the bridge daily 5am–6pm, during Daylight Savings Time until 9pm. $6 auto toll, southbound only.

Prepare to be amazed. The Golden Gate Bridge is truly astonishing. The balletic lines. The massive strength. The beautiful color. The staggering backdrop of sea and fog, craggy headlands and rocky shore and, in the distance, the little pastel outpost that is San Francisco . . . It's no wonder the Golden Gate Bridge is one of the most photographed manmade structures on earth.

How did it come to be? The idea for a bridge over the narrow, treacherous strait where the San Francisco Bay meets the Pacific Ocean was first proposed in 1869 but dismissed over the ensuing four decades as unnecessary, structurally impossible and too expensive. By the early 20C, however, Marin County commuters started grumbling for an alternative to the ferry. In 1918 San Francisco's board of supervisors commissioned a feasibility study, but they balked at the proposed designs' price tags: some as high as $100 million. Enter Joseph Strauss, an experienced engineer who had already built more than 400 bridges around the world. When he said the job could be done for $27 million, people believed him, and public support for the project began to build.

Ground was broken in 1933, and for the next four years, thousands

How the Golden Gate Bridge Measures Up

Height – The roadway hangs 220ft over the water at high tide; the towers are 746ft (65 stories) tall. The towers above the water are 746ft tall and the towers above the roadway are 500ft tall."

Length – The bridge measures 6,450ft (1.7mi) from end to end; the clear span between the towers is 4,200ft (1.22mi).

Strength – The two main cables, which are anchored in place by 240-million-pound concrete blocks on either side of the bridge, measure 36 3/8 inches in diameter and comprise 80,000mi of wire. The bridge contains a whopping 1.66 billion pounds of steel.

of men labored on the bridge, sinking its piers and anchorages into bedrock; erecting its two massive steel towers; draping three-foot-thick cables across the span; and building, piece by piece, the roadway to be suspended from those cables. Eleven men died during construction, but stringent safety procedures likely saved many others. The Golden Gate Bridge, which ended up costing $35 million, was inaugurated on May 27, 1937, to universal acclaim.

View of Lombard Street

©Kevin Connors/Dreamstime.com

Lombard Street★★★

Between Hyde & Leavenworth Sts. See For Fun.

In 1847, at a time when the city had one school and one newspaper

and about 800 residents, Mayor Washington A. Bartlett hired Irish engineer Jasper O'Farrell to draw up a town plan. O'Farrell traced a rectangular grid over the peninsula, completely ignoring the city's extreme topography. Developers were left to fend for themselves if they wanted to build

Steep San Francisco

While Lombard Street is often called the "**crookedest street in the world**," Vermont Street's seven sharp switchbacks near McKinley Square make it the city's actual crookedest street. The twisty section hosts an annual Bring Your Own Big Wheel race each spring.

San Francisco's many steep hills are also famed for the hundreds of public stairways that traverse them, offering quiet nooks, lush gardens and incredible views. Russian Hill's Vallejo Steps *(between Mason and Taylor)* offer prime views of the Bay Bridge and Alcatraz; nearby, a wooden staircase climbs to the secluded Macondray Lane. Pacific Heights' Lyon Steps *(between Vallejo St. and Broadway)* serve as a lovely alternative to a gym workout, and the Sunset District's stunning Moraga Steps *(15th Ave. and Moraga St.)* feature a gorgeous tiled mosaic created by neighborhood residents.

LANDMARKS

Steepest Blocks of San Francisco

- Filbert between Hyde & Leavenworth (Russian Hill): 31.5% grade
- Jones between Union & Filbert (Russian Hill): 29% grade
- Duboce between Buena Vista & Alpine (Haight-Ashbury): 27.9% grade
- Lombard between Hyde & Leavenworth (Russian Hill): 27% grade
- Jones between Green & Union (Russian Hill): 26% grade
- Webster between Vallejo & Broadway (Pacific Heights): 26% grade
- Duboce between Alpine & Castro (Haight-Ashbury): 25% grade
- Jones between Pine & California (Nob Hill): 24.8% grade
- Fillmore between Vallejo & Broadway (Pacific Heights): 24% grade

high into the hills. The cable car, invented in 1873, was the principal means of conquering hills without leveling them, but serpentine Lombard Street is pretty clever too. Its eight switchbacks, laid out in cobblestones in 1922, reduce the block's natural 27 percent grade to a workable 16 percent.

Bay Bridge★★

I-80 between San Francisco and Oakland. $4-6 toll depending on day and time, westbound only.

Long considered the ugly little sister of the Golden Gate Bridge, the San Francisco-Oakland Bay Bridge (1936) is undergoing an extensive redesign to make it safer, more attractive, and accessible to bicycle traffic and pedestrians.

Due to the tremendous distance it must span—8.5mi—the bridge has always consisted of two sections. The western section—two suspension bridges set end to end—that links San Francisco to Yerba Buena Island will remain untouched. In January 2002 work began on converting the east span, a chunky, cantilever-truss bridge between the island and Oakland, into an elegant, more flexible suspension bridge. The bridge's two levels will be replaced by a single, wider roadway, not only avoiding the "sandwiching" effect that happened when the top level collapsed in the 1989 Loma Prieta earthquake (killing 63 people), but also allowing all drivers panoramic views of the San Francisco skyline and the East Bay hills.

Bay Bridge at night

©PhotoDisc, Inc.

City Hall★★

Civic Center, bounded by Grove, McAllister, Polk & Van Ness Sts. 415-554-4000. www.sfgov.org/site/cityhall_index.asp. Open year-round Mon–Fri 8am–8pm. Closed major holidays. Free docent-led tours held Mon–Fri 10am, 12pm and 2pm. Call 415-554-6139.

City Hall

Brigitta L. House/MICHELIN

One of the only remnants of Daniel Burnham's plan to turn San Francisco into a "city beautiful," with grand Classical structures lording over spoked streets and prim, stately parks, City Hall (1915) is an impressive four-story building covering two city blocks. Its most distinguished feature is its regal dome, which is trimmed in gold-leaf and rises 13ft taller than that of the US Capitol in Washington, DC. The rows of Doric pillars and colonnades are typical of the Beaux-Arts style favored by its architect, Arthur Brown Jr. Within, a spiraling marble staircase ascends to a spectacular 181ft open rotunda.

Alamo Square's Painted Ladies

The row of Victorians located at 710-720 Steiner St., between Hayes and Grove Streets, strikes a familiar chord with most San Francisco visitors. One of the most photographed vantages in the city, **Postcard Row★★★** stands before a remarkable, snapshot-ready backdrop featuring many city landmarks, including the Transamerica Pyramid. Lush, grassy Alamo Square Park, across the street, conveniently allows photographers ample time to focus. Distinguished externally by window and door treatments

Swensen's Ice Cream

Union Street at Hyde Street. 415-775-6818. San Franciscans don't cope well with hot weather. So when native son Earle Swensen found himself on a troop ship in the South Pacific during World War II, he volunteered to make ice cream to cool the men down. Afterward he returned to his hometown and perfected his recipe at this, the flagship of Swensen's over 300-strong fleet of ice-cream parlors.

and by color, the three-story, wooden, gable-roofed houses were completed in 1895 and sold for $3,500 a piece by Irish-born carpenter and real-estate developer Matthew Kavanagh. All seven homes are private, one- or two-family dwellings.

Around 48,000 houses were built in the Victorian and Edwardian styles in San Francisco between 1849 and 1915. Many were destroyed in the 1906 earthquake.

LANDMARKS

43

Ferry Building Farmers' Market

Market St. at The Embarcadero. Open year-round Tue 10am–2pm & Sat 8am–2pm. 415-291-3276. www.ferryplazafarmersmarket.com. The city's most prestigious farmers' market brings together Bay Area farmers and artisnal food producers two days a week year-round. Chef tours, farmer interviews, live music, and cooking demonstrations are regular fixtures on the scene. After perusing the goodies outside, head indoors, where the crème de la creme of the Bay Area's artisan food producers maintain outlets. Try Cowgirl Creamery for cheeses, Prather Ranch Meat Company for humanely raised meats, Acme Bread Company for fresh loaves, and Frog Hollow Farms for jellies and conserves.

Ferry Building★★

Embarcadero at Market St. 415-693-0996. www.ferrybuilding marketplace.com. Open Mon–Fri 10am–6pm, Sat 9am–6pm, Sun 11am–5pm. Extended hours in summer.

The hugely successful Ferry Building renovation, completed in 2004, has brought this long-neglected landmark back into the spotlight as an airy retail and restaurant complex. Designed by A. Page Brown, the 1898 steel-reinforced sandstone structure is distinguished by its 244ft clock tower. During the peak years of ferry service, in the early 1930s, nearly 50,000 people passed through the vaulted nave each day. That number plummeted upon the opening of the bridges in 1936 and 1937, though, and slowly the building fell into disuse. The 1957 construction of the elevated Embarcadero Freeway effectively severed the Ferry Building from the Financial District for 35 years. Damaged by the 1989 earthquake, the highway was dismantled and the Ferry Building was returned to its former grandeur. It now shines as the city's premier showcase for local produce and gourmet goodies (see Must Shop and Musts for Fun).

Filbert Steps★★

Filbert Street, between Sansome Street and Coit Tower.

Concrete and wooden stairs, descending this steep section of Filbert Street, comprise one of the city's most charming and surprising pathways. At 1360 Montgomery Street (1937), the stairs pass a gleaming Streamline

Ferry Building

Brigitta L. House/MICHELIN

Moderne apartment house that appeared in the 1947 film *Dark Passage*, starring Humphrey Bogart. Below Montgomery Street, the wooden staircase climbs through lushly landscaped garden terraces of mid-19C cottages. Keep your ears peeled for Telegraph Hill's vocal colonies of colorful parrots, descendants of household pets who escaped domestication.

🚃 St. Francis Hotel★★

335 Powell St., Union Square.
415-397-7000. www.westin.com.
See Must Stay.

San Francisco's second-oldest hotel was built overlooking Union Square by railroad baron Charles Crocker, who felt his city needed world-class accommodations. The hotel even survived the 1906 earthquake intact, but the ensuing fire gutted the interior. No matter. It was quickly rebuilt (and enlarged), opening in 1907. It has been a magnet for bigwigs ever since. Hemingway hunkered down here. So did Queen Elizabeth II, the Shah of Iran, and all US presidents since Taft. Step inside to ogle the entrance hall, with its coffered ceilings, travertine marble

and ornate balconies. The Magneta grandfather clock has long been a favorite rendezvous point for city socialites.

Palace of Fine Arts★★

Baker & Beach Sts.
www.exploratorium.edu/palace.

Roman ruins in San Francisco? You might think so when you see the Palace of Fine Arts with its grand open rotunda. The rotunda is your clue to recognizing this well-known landmark, whether you're cruising the bay, visiting the Golden Gate Bridge, or shopping in the Marina district where the Palace is located. Architect Bernard Maybeck designed the Palace to house art exhibits for the Panama-Pacific International Exposition of 1915 (see previous page).

The building, distinguished by its 110ft-high-by-135ft-wide rotunda and surrounding colonnade, was only designed to last two years. Framed in wood, steel and chicken-wire, the Palace was covered with a plaster and burlap-fiber mixture called "staff". The structure's surface was then sprayed to look like travertine marble.

The Panama-Pacific International Exposition of 1915

San Franciscans, rejuvenated by their city's resurrection from the 1906 earthquake and fire, and eagerly anticipating the completion of the Panama Canal, sought a way to celebrate that would also draw attention away from Los Angeles, their chief competitor in the shipping industry. Their answer was the Panama-Pacific International Exposition. With a collection of pavilions designed by some of the era's best architects, the exposition represented 25 countries and 29 states. An airplane could fly through the Great Palace of Machinery, and the Oregon state pavilion stood as a redwood Parthenon. More than 20 million people visited the fair in its 10 months of operation. Today, only the Marina Yacht Harbor and the Palace of Fine Arts stand as remnants of this grand affair.

LANDMARKS

45

Palace of Fine Arts

©PhotoDisc, Inc.

When the fair buildings were torn down to make way for residential development, aesthetically minded citizens lobbied to spare the Palace of Fine Arts. No efforts were made to shore up the building, however, and it slowly disintegrated until a plan to restore it was initiated in 1962. By making casts of each column and detail, and then razing the old sections, the building was entirely reconstructed from concrete and steel between 1964 and 1967. Today the rotunda, with its eight large relief panels illustrating Greek culture, is mirrored in the waters of the duck pond at its feet.

Exploratorium★★

3601 Lyon St., behind the Palace of Fine Arts rotunda. See For Kids.

Transamerica Pyramid★★

600 Montgomery St. between Washington & Clay Sts.
thepyramidcenter.com

Though it lords over the Financial District in imperial fashion, San Francisco's tallest building is not,

in fact, its tallest structure—that designation goes to Sutro Tower, a two-pronged television transmitter perched atop the city's highest peak. But the Transamerica Pyramid is without a doubt the more distinctive landmark.

Rising 48 stories to a crisp white point, it was designed by the Los Angeles firm of William Pereira and Associates in 1969 and completed in 1972. San Franciscans grumbled about the structure at first, feeling it ostentatious and too modern for their quaint little burg, but now it's

Transamerica Pyramid

Phillip H. Coblentz/SFCVB

Jackson Square★★

Bounded by Washington, Montgomery & Sansome Sts., and Pacific Ave.
Venture north of the pyramid to one of San Francisco's oldest districts, a tiny enclave of two- and three-story brick buildings that miraculously survived the 1906 earthquake and fire; many date back to the 1850s. Pacific Avenue was for years the city's rowdiest street, crammed as it was with saloons, dance halls, gambling parlors, brothels and boarding houses for transient sailors. Time has mellowed the neighborhood, which is now one of the city's premier destinations for buying art and antiques. *(http://www.jacksonsquaresf.com)*

roundly hailed as an architectural gem. The pyramid was specially designed to withstand earthquakes and tremors. Though built on landfill, not bedrock, it has a 52ft-deep steel and concrete foundation that moves with quakes, and a unique truss system to support the upper stories. At the 29th floor, two concrete wings rise vertically from the structure's tapering walls to accommodate elevator shafts that otherwise would have cut into the precious high-floor office space. A single private conference room on the 48th floor boasts 360-degree views of the city and the bay. A hollow lantern takes up the top 212ft of the pyramid.

Virtual Visit – Unfortunately, due to security concerns, the general public is not allowed inside the Transamerica Pyramid at this time.

However, a street-level "virtual observation deck" has been set up on Washington Street. There you can look down at the city via rooftop cameras. Better yet, take a seat in adjacent Redwood Park, a pleasant, half-acre grove of some 40 redwood trees, and look up.

🌲 Crissy Field

Crissy Field Ave. off Lincoln Blvd, Marina.

A bayshore airfield from 1919 to 1936, Crissy Field has since been restored to tidal marsh, beach and dunes by the National Park Service. Today, the dirt trail running through it, along the northern waterfront to the base of the Golden Gate, is one of the most popular places in the city for jogging and casual bike-riding.

Anchor Brewing Company

1705 Mariposa St. (at De Haro St.). 415-863-8350. www.anchorbrewing.com. Free tour offered twice daily on weekdays. Reservations required; book as soon as possible, up to 6 months in advance. Here's where the whole microbrew movement started. Founded in 1896, Anchor began as one of many local breweries, but Prohibition and the decline of manufacturing that followed threatened to close its doors. Appliance heir Fritz Maytag bought the company in 1965 and perfected its tar amber ale after visiting breweries throughout Europe. Beer drinkers used to thin, flavorless lagers took to the stronger taste, and entrepreneurs nationwide copied Maytag's model. The extremely popular two-hour tour explains all aspects of production and ends with samples of each Anchor brew made (six and counting).

MUSEUMS

Maybe you didn't come to the City by the Bay to visit museums. Sure, there's a ton of other things to do, but you'd be remiss if you didn't at least sample the city's cultural offerings. There's much for art lovers here, from the acclaimed Asian Art Museum to SF MOMA. And the Cable Car Museum and the Exploratorium are musts for younger visitors.

Asian Art Museum★★★

200 Larkin St., Civic Center. 415-581-3500. www.asianart.org. Open year-round Tue–Sun 10am–5pm (Thu until 9pm, Feb-Oct). Closed Mon, Jan 1, Thanksgiving and Dec 25. $12. Free admission the first Sun of every month.

338 Buddha, Asian Art Museum

Kaz Tsuruta/Asian Art Museum

Don't miss this star among San Francisco's diverse museums. The group of some 15,000 works owned by the Asian Art Museum spans 6,000 years and constitutes the largest museum in the US devoted to Asian art. Objects run the gamut from Chinese jades to Japanese kimonos and Islamic manuscripts to Korean celadons. The museum was born in 1959, when Chicago millionaire Avery Brundage offered San Francisco a part of his vast collection of Asian art on the condition that the city build a museum to display it. Completed in 1966, the Asian Art Museum was located for 35 years in Golden Gate Park. Having long outgrown its original home, the museum opened in its spectacular new digs in the renovated 1917 Beaux-Arts-style San Francisco Public Library in March 2003. The expansive 29,000sq ft of gallery space is twice as big as the original museum, allowing for the display of some 2,500 artworks from the permanent collection.

AsiaAlive

Drop by the museum's Grand Hall, the sumptuous former catalog room of the library, which is set off by a barrel-vaulted and coffered travertine marble ceiling, for interactive programs that focus on the diverse arts of Asia. Here's your chance to learn Afghan knotted-pile rug weaving or traditional Chinese painting techniques from experts in the arts—the theme changes each month. This is fun for the whole family, where you can meet the artists and watch them demonstrate their craft, then try your own hand at designing a miniature rug or creating a Chinese brush painting. Best of all, it's free. *Programs are offered daily in the second-floor Samsung Hall from 12pm–4pm (extended hours on Thu evenings).*

MUST SEE

Home Is Where The Art Is

The remarkable setting for this stellar collection was designed by Italian architect **Gae Aulenti**, whose credits include the Musée d'Orsay in Paris. She transformed the gloomy former library into a dramatic display space centering on an open sky-lit court. In the process, Aulenti preserved the historic building's prominent elements, such as the original marble staircase, columned loggia and great hall. One-third of $160 million spent on the renovation of the library building went to retrofit the structure in case of an earthquake. To protect its priceless collection, the whole museum now floats on an underground moat. If an earthquake were to shake the city, the building would move as one unit, gently balanced in the water.

A glass-enclosed escalator now whisks visitors up to the third floor where they work their way down through the 33 galleries on two floors that display objects from the permanent collection. Presented as the story of Asian culture, the collection is organized geographically (each region claims a different-colored gallery) and thematically—according to the spread of Buddhism, trade and interchange, and local beliefs and customs. In each room, artworks are displayed chronologically, from the oldest to the most recent. Eye-catching objects are placed in the middle of the galleries as visual lures to lead you into the next room. Back on the ground floor, you'll find changing exhibits, an upscale museum shop, and Café Asia, featuring such pan-Asian fare as Bento boxes, sushi, noodle dishes, hot pots and rice bowls.

Highlights of the Collection
Free multilingual audio tours are available to introduce you to the museum's highlights. Here's a small taste to whet your appetite:

338 Buddha★★★ – The museum's prize, this small bronze statue is the oldest dated Chinese Buddha in existence; 338 refers to the year it was made.
Rhino ritual vessel★★ – This Shang Dynasty bronze vessel is unique for its animal shape.

Rhino Ritual Vessel, Asian Art Museum

Kaz Tsuruta/Asian Art Museum

Elephant throne★★ – The stunning silver throne was made in India c.1870–1920.

Indonesian rod puppets★★ – The museum's vivid set of 71 rod puppets is a rare find.

An authentic Japanese tea room★ – on the second floor hosts tea ceremonies once a month (be sure to make reservations well in advance as attendance is limited).

Cable Car Museum★★

1201 Mason St. at Washington St. 415-474-1887. www.cablecar museum.org. Open daily Apr–Sept 10am–6pm. Rest of the year daily 10am–5pm. Closed Jan 1, Thanksgiving Day & Dec 25.

San Francisco's cable-car system is the only one of its kind in the world, and this is the place to see it in action. Besides being a museum, the weathered brick building on the steep north slope of Nob Hill does double duty as the cable-car barn and powerhouse for the city's fabled cable cars.

Head to the upper level, where you can stand on the balcony and gape at the thrumming cable-car mechanism. Each of the three cable lines in existence today has its own machinery here: a 510-horsepower DC electric motor, gears to control the speed of the motor, and a set of three huge pulleys, called sheaves. To keep the cable from slipping, each cable wraps around a set of powered sheave wheels and over and under unpowered wheels in a figure-8 pattern.

Downstairs, you'll find historic photographs and displays explaining how the cable cars came to be, as well as Car No. 8, the only surviving vehicle from the city's first cable-car line (1873). You can even ring a real cable-car bell—the sound that's synonymous with San Francisco. And don't leave the city without riding on a cable car (*see For Fun*).

California Academy of Sciences★★

55 Concourse Dr. Golden Gate Park. Open year-round Mon–Sat 9:30am –5pm, Sun 11am–5pm. Closed Thanksgiving Day, Dec 25. Adult $29.95. 415-379-8000. www.calacademy.org

The oldest scientific institution in the West, the venerable California

---

Getting A Grip

Today's **cable car** system uses the mechanism developed in 1873 by Scottish immigrant Andrew Hallidie, who came to California in 1852 to build a wire-rope transport system for the gold mines. Just as a constantly moving tow rope pulls a skier up a snowy slope, huge loops of steel cable run a continuous 9.5mph beneath Powell, Hyde, Mason and California streets. The cable is powered by electric motors at the Cable Car Barn (*above*). To start the car moving, the "gripman" stands in the middle of the car and "throws" a lever that extends down through a slot in the street. At the underground end of the lever, a "grip" closes and opens like a jaw on the moving cable. The tighter the grip closes, the faster the car goes. To reduce speed, the gripman opens the grip to release the cable; he applies brakes to stop. A conductor at the rear of the car helps with braking when necessary.

Rainforests of the World exhibit, California Academy of Sciences

©Tim Griffith/California Academy of Sciences

Academy of Sciences has since its inception aimed to explore, explain and celebrate the natural world. Founded in 1853 in a surge of post-Gold Rush enthusiasm for knowledge about California's physical environment, the Academy of Sciences began as a clubby group of naturalists who collected specimens, presented scholarly papers, and eventually began to function as a natural history museum.

Today, the academy's three branches—the Kimball Natural History Museum, the Steinhart Aquarium and the Morrison Planetarium—occupy a groundbreaking new building that showcases institutional philosophy and cutting-edge technology along with the academy's legendary and ever-expanding collections.

The academy's 20 million scientific specimens—including insects, scorpions, reptiles, amphibians and thousands of fish—occupy displays that teach visitors about the incredible variety of earth's environments. Kids will especially love the Africa Hall, with its pod

The Academy's New Home

Pritzker Prize–winning architect **Renzo Piano** (whose credits include the Centre Georges Pompidou in Paris) was engaged to design a building integrating all three branches of the Academy under one roof. A hallmark of Piano's 410,000sq ft, $400 million structure is a "living roof" made up of native California plants and photovoltaic cells. This unique lid not only helps the building meld with its surroundings, but also absorbs rainwater to decrease runoff and provides natural insulation.

of 20 South African penguins, the swamp exhibit with its underwater viewing panels; and Rainforests of the World, a 4-story glass sphere in the central courtyard that takes visitors from understory to canopy to root systems.

From here an acrylic tunnel passes through the Amazon River exhibit to the Aquarium, featuring an extraordinary living coral reef with 4,000 fish.

MUSEUMS

California Palace of the Legion of Honor★★

100 34th Ave. at Clement St., in Lincoln Park. 415-863-3330. legionofhonor.famsf.org. Open year-round Tue–Sun 9:30am-5:15pm. Closed Jan 1, Thanksgiving and Dec 25. Adults $10; free first Tuesday of every month. Admission tickets to the Legion of Honor include same-day admission to the de Young.

Overlooking the Pacific Ocean from its remote perch aptly called Land's End, the Legion of Honor displays 4,000 years of ancient and European art. And what more fitting place to see splendid artwork than in architect George Applegarth's three-quarter-scale concrete version of the 18C Palais de la Légion d'Honneur in Paris? Founded by Alma and Adolph Spreckels, the Legion was dedicated on Armistice Day 1924 in honor of the 3,600 Californians who perished in World War I. In 1995 the Legion underwent a three-year overhaul and seismic retrofitting that added an underground level and six new special-exhibition galleries surrounding a skylit court. Today its collection of some 83,750 objects includes European masterworks from the 14C to the 20C, European decorative arts, and antiquities from the ancient Mediterranean world and the Near East.

- In 1950 the Legion received the city-owned **Achenbach Foundation for Graphic Arts**, which includes more than 70,000 prints, drawings, and illustrated books spanning six centuries.
- The **Legion of Honor** owns 111 Rodin sculptures, which founder Alma Spreckels—who knew the sculptor personally—collected during Rodin's lifetime. You can see an original cast of Rodin's Thinker in the Court of Honor.

Contemporary Jewish Museum

736 Mission St., between 3rd and 4th streets. Fri–Tue 11am-5pm, Thu 1–8pm. Closed Jan 1, July 4, Thanksgiving, and major Jewish holidays. $10. 415-655-7800. www.cjm.org.

This award-winning museum mounts several exhibitions per year to promote understanding of Jewish culture through contemporary art. Established in 1984, it maintains strong community ties via ongoing educational programs. The $50 million renovation of its new home (opened in 2008), the Jessie Street Power Substation, was overseen by renowned architect Daniel Libeskind.

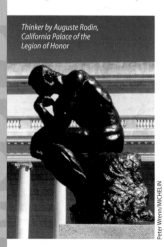

Thinker by Auguste Rodin, California Palace of the Legion of Honor

Peter Wrenn/MICHELIN

Art Patron With Attitude

Born in San Francisco to impoverished European immigrants, **Alma de Bretteville** (1881–1968) inherited the energy of her hard-working mother and the pride of her father, a descendant of the faded nobility of the French de Bretteville lineage, who instilled in his daughter a sense of noblesse oblige. Alma grew into a statuesque, willful, mostly self-educated woman who defied convention in many ways. After several years of a socially unacknowledged liaison, she married sugar magnate Adolph Spreckels in 1908.

In 1914 she met and fell under the influence of American-born dancer Löie Fuller, the toast of Belle Epoque Paris, who convinced Alma that her destiny was to become a great patron of the arts with Löie as her chief advisor. Alma took Löie's challenge to heart and in 1915, she convinced her husband to build a new art museum in San Francisco.

Exploratorium★★

3601 Lyon St., at the Palace of Fine Arts (see Landmarks). 415-561-0399. www.exploratorium.edu. Open year-round Tue–Sun 10am–5pm. Closed Mon, Thanksgiving Day & Dec 25. $12 adults, $9.50 youth (ages 13–17), $8 children (ages 4–12). Free the first Wed of each month.

Since 1969 the Exploratorium has helped visitors to discover science at their own pace. Science comes to life in hundreds of interactive stations inside the Palace of Fine Arts. By pushing buttons, rotating wheels, peering through prisms, and performing a host of other actions, you set experiments in motion and observe the results. Among the displays in physics, electricity, life science, weather, linguistics, sense perception and more, the Seeing and Traits of Life areas have been reconfigured to incorporate new research and revitalized exhibits. If you're not claustrophobic, try crawling through the multilevel Tactile Dome; inside it's pitch-black and soundproof, so you have to feel your way through.

de Young Museum★★

50 Hagiwara Tea Garden Drive at John F. Kennedy Dr., in Golden Gate Park. 415-750-3600; deyoung.famsf.org. Open year-round Tue-Sun 9:30am-5:15pm, and Friday mid-Jan–Nov until 8:45pm. Closed Jan 1, Thanksgiving and Dec 25. Adults $10; free first Tuesday of every month. Admission tickets to the de Young include same-day admission to the Legion of Honor.

The de Young is today a major force on the West Coast museum scene. Its collection from the pre-Columbian era to the present traces the history of art in the Americas, complemented by significant holding in textiles, African and Oceanic art.

The de Young owes its existence to its namesake, Michael H. de Young, co-founder of the *San Francisco Chronicle*, who founded the museum in 1895. Collecting with more enthusiasm than knowledge, de Young amassed a hodgepodge of artwork, historic artifacts and natural-history exhibits that was described at one point as consisting of "23,000 stuffed birds

de Young Museum

and eggs of every biped that ever had wings." Eventually, though, de Young attracted the attention of benefactors such as John D. Rockefeller, whose gift of American paintings and works on paper in 1978 propelled the museum to first-class status.

American Art★★ – Eighteen galleries are devoted to the museum's extensive collection of more than 1,000 paintings by American artists, from colonial times to the 20C.

Art of the Americas★ – Ancient objects from Mesoamerica, Central and South America, and the West Coast of North America make up the heart of this collection, which includes Teotihuacán murals and a 10ft totem pole from Alaska.

African Art – This rapidly growing collection highlights a cross-section of sub-Saharan cultures and illustrates some of the oldest traditions in art.

Oceanic Art – The museum's holdings of Oceanic art come from Melanesia, Indonesia, Polynesia, the Caroline Islands of Micronesia, and the Maori peoples of New Zealand.

Textiles – This collection includes more than 12,000 textiles and costumes from around the world, from Turkish carpets to the latest couture.

The New de Young

Funded by $190 million in private donations, the daring three-story de Young building was created by Swiss architects **Jacques Herzog** and **Pierre de Meuron**, designers of London's Tate Modern. A total of 950,000 pounds of copper sheaths the exterior; over the course of the next decade it will fade from bright copper to cinnamon, then to a rich green that will blend in with the surrounding trees. The interior is centered on a vast, airy lobby, with selections from the permanent collection displayed in galleries on the Concourse and Upper levels. Descend to the basement for special exhibits and a gift store, or ascend to the 144ft tower's Observation Deck for sweeping 360-degree views.

San Francisco Museum of Modern Art★★

[M9] refers to map on front inside cover. 151 3rd St. 415-357-4000. www.sfmoma.org. Open Memorial Day–Labor Day Thu–Tue 10am–5:45pm. Rest of the year Thu–Tue 11am–5:45pm (Thu until 8:45pm). Closed Wed & major holidays. $18 for adults, $12 for seniors and $9 for students. Kids 12 and under are FREE.

SF MOMA, as it's known, stands out for its eye-catching architecture as much as for its collection. You can pick the museum out from the South of Market skyline by its signature 125ft-tall cylindrical tower. Swiss architect Mario Botta slanted the top of the cylinder toward Third Street and faced the angled surface with glass in order to create a huge skylight that floods the upper galleries with natural light. Rows of black and white granite on the shaft contrast with the red brick of Botta's post-Modern museum building. Founded in 1935, San Francisco's premier showcase for modern art moved into its new digs in 1995 in the burgeoning Yerba Buena Arts District. In the stunning **central atrium★★**, lined with alternating bands of polished and unpolished black marble, you can climb the central staircase to the gallery floors. On the second floor, selections from the museum's permanent collection of more than 26,000 works illustrate the diversity of contemporary art. The third, fourth and fifth floors host special exhibitions.

The Buena Vista

2765 Hyde St. at the corner of Hyde & Beach Sts. 415-474-5044. www.thebuenavista.com. A short two-block walk east of the National Maritime Museum will bring you to a San Francisco institution: the **Buena Vista Cafe.** Known as the first bar in the US to serve Irish coffee (a heady concoction of Irish whiskey, coffee and whipped cream), this amiable bar sold its first steaming mug of brew in 1952. Go for a quick breakfast or lunch, or better yet, stop in after dinner for one of its signature spiked coffee drinks—the Buena Vista is open every day until 2am.

Richard Barnes/SFMOMA

Atrium, San Francisco Museum of Modern Art

MUSEUMS

Museum of Craft and Folk Art

Museum of Craft and Folk Art

If you're not afraid of heights, venture across the fifth floor's dramatic 35ft-long steel **bowstring-truss bridge★**, suspended at a dizzying 75ft above the lobby. You'll find changing exhibits in a room at the other end.

Highlights of the Permanent Collection

Painting and Sculpture – Begin your introduction to this stellar group of 20C and 21C works with Matisse—don't miss his seminal *Femme au chapeau (Woman with a Hat)*, and move on to Picasso,

Klee, Dalí, de Kooning, Motherwell, Rauschenberg and more.

Architecture and Design – Frequently rotating shows of furniture, graphic arts and building design are tapped from the permanent collection.

Photography – The museum's distinguished group of images dates from the 1840s to the present.

Museum of Craft and Folk Art

51 Yerba Buena Lane, Wed–Sat 11am–6pm. Closed major holidays. Adults $5. 415-227-4888. www.mocfa.org.

The only folk art museum in Northern California, the Museum of Craft and Folk Art presents focused and innovative exhibits of traditional and contemporary folk art and craft from around the world. The store stocks an excellent selection of pottery, glassware, jewelry and other items by local artisans. The museum shop is a great place to pick up crafts made by local artists.

Edible Art

Situated in the San Francisco Museum of Art is the **Caffè Museo** *(415-357-4500; Closed Wed; www.caffemuseo.com)* which serves a Mediterranean-inspired menu for lunch—and for dinner on Thursday, when the museum is open late.
The kitchen cooks up a different seasonal soup or stew every day; breads and pastries are baked on-site.

National Maritime Museum★

[M6] refers to map on front inside cover. Beach St. at Polk St. 415-447-5000. http://www.nps.gov/safr/historyculture/bathhousebuilding.htm. Open year-round daily 10am–4pm. Closed Jan 1, Thanksgiving Day & Dec 25.

It's hard to mistake this big, white, ship-shaped building in the Fisherman's Wharf area. The 1939 Streamline Moderne-style museum, with its deck railings and porthole windows, looks just like an ocean liner berthed at the edge of the bay.

Part of the **San Francisco Maritime National Historical Park★**, the museum is located near the Hyde Street Pier historical ships that also fall under the park's umbrella. It was built as the Aquatic Park Casino, the intended centerpiece of a never-realized recreational complex built by the Works Progress Administration.

From 1941 to 1948 the building was a military base, with troops placed there during World War II. It later became home to the San Francisco Maritime Museum. Re-opened in 2010 following a multi-year rehabilitation of the building and adjacent bleachers, the museum is now planning new exhibits; already installed are several ship models, paintings, and dioramas.

Inside the lobby, be sure to take note of Hilaire Hiler's expressionistic undersea murals, which have been restored. Go out on the upper deck for **great views★★** of the historical ships on Hyde Street Pier, the Golden Gate Bridge and the Marin Headlands.

San Francisco Art Institute★

800 Chestnut St., between Jones & Leavenworth Sts. 415-771-7020. www.sfai.edu. Gallery hours vary (see below).

A cultural center as well as a fine-arts college, the Art Institute was established in 1871 to foster understanding of contemporary art and to educate the leading artists of the time. The institute has attracted a wealth of forward thinkers in its time; alumni include Pulitzer Prize-winning cartoonist Rube Goldberg, painter Richard Diebenkorn, photographer Annie Liebovitz as well as the late Grateful Dead guitarist Jerry Garcia.

Today the institute enrolls about 650 students and welcomes the public to its Spanish Colonial Revival-style campus near Russian Hill to view thought-provoking exhibits, attend lectures by local and visiting international artists, and watch the latest in avant-garde films.

Walter and McBean Galleries – *415-749-4563. Open year-round Tue–Sat 11am–6pm.* The school's

---

Art Institute Cafe

415-749-4567. Closed weekends. Wind your way through the art- and handbill-lined hallways to the institute's broad back deck. Grab a sandwich or a daily entrée—guaranteed to fill starving artists at rock-bottom prices—and sit back and relax. The foreground of congregating students against a stunning backdrop of city, bay and sky may inspire you to bring out your brushes.

MUSEUMS

Quad, San Francisco Art Institute

main exhibition galleries showcase a year-round schedule of photographs, paintings, installations and other work by both local and international artists. The focus here is on newly commissioned art.

Diego Rivera Gallery – *415-771-7020, ext. 4410. Open year-round Mon–Sat daily 9am–5pm.*

This chapel-like gallery features *The Making of a Fresco Showing the Building of a City* (1931) by the famed Mexican artist Diego Rivera (1886–1957). Rivera himself is pictured in the two-story mural, along with his wife, artist Frida Kahlo. Exhibitions of student work here change weekly.

Wells Fargo History Museum★

420 Montgomery St. 415-396-2619. www.wellsfargohistory.com. Open year-round Mon–Fri 9am–5pm. Closed major holidays.

Precursor to our modern-day overnight delivery services, Wells Fargo & Co. prided itself on its fast delivery of gold, mail and valuables when it was founded in 1852. Today the company operates as a bank, but in the company's museum you can relive the Old West days when villains like Black Bart robbed the stagecoaches. Kids will want to head straight for the mezzanine, where they can sit on a jostling

© *Wells Fargo History Museum*

reconstructed Concord coach and listen to a recorded description of a harrowing cross-country journey of the 1850s. Other exhibits tell the story of the Gold Rush days through photographs, letters, and glittering gold nuggets.

Museums at Fort Mason

At Fort Mason Center. Entrance on Marina Blvd. at Buchanan St. 415-345-7544. www.fortmason.org.

This former military base now houses a host of museums and galleries (*see Historic Sites*).
San Francisco Museum of Modern Art Artists Gallery – *Bldg. A. Tue-Sat 11:30am–5:30pm. Closed Jan 1, July 4, Thanksgiving weekend, and Christmas week. 415-441-4777. www.sfmoma.org.* Sister to SF MOMA, the gallery displays rotating contemporary art exhibits and has given many local artists their start.
Museo ItaloAmericano – *Bldg. C. Open year-round Tue-Sun noon-4pm. Closed major holidays. Free admission. 415-673-2200. www.museoitaloamericano.org.* A permanent collection of modern

Italian and Italian-American art is featured here.

Yerba Buena Center for the Arts★

701 Mission Street, at Third Street. Thu–Sat noon–8pm, Sun noon–6pm, first Tues of month (free) noon–8pm. Closed major holidays. Adults $7. 415-978-2787. www.ybca.org.

Exploring such issues as race, class, gender, history, technology and art itself, the changing exhibitions in this low-slung, modernistic building (1993, Fumihiko Maki) reflect the cultural diversity and experimental élan of the Bay Area. The $44 million structure contains a 6,700sq ft performance space, two cavernous first floor galleries, and a sculpture plaza. Upstairs, a high-tech gallery accommodates film, video and multimedia installations. YBCA's two buildings include galleries, a flexible "Forum" space, a film/video screening room designed by Fumihiko Maki in association with RMW, and the Novellus Theater.

Yerba Buena Center for the Arts

©Rafael Ramirez Lee/Dreamstime.com

HISTORIC SITES

San Francisco savors its long and baudy history. Thanks to public and private preservation efforts, you can glimpse the lives of the city's first settlers, honor the soldiers—Spanish, Mexican and American—who protected the city in times of war, and immerse yourself in the opulence of bygone days.

The Presidio★★

Access via Lincoln Blvd., Lombard St. (at Lyon St.), Presidio Blvd. (at Pacific St.) or Arguello Blvd. (at Pacific St.). 415-561-4323. www.nps.gov/prsf. For visitor center hours, see sidebar, below.

History with a view? You bet! Perched atop 1,480 acres overlooking the Golden Gate Bridge, the Presidio may be the most beautiful military installation in the US. The adobe quadrangle called the Presidio (Spanish for "military garrison") was built as a Spanish outpost in 1776, predating Mission Dolores by a month. Largely ignored by Spanish officials and plagued by decades of rain, earthquakes, wind and salt air, the fort was crumbling when the

Tips for Visiting

Start your visit to this often fog-shrouded point at the **Presidio Visitor Center** on the Main Post *(50 Morago Ave., in the Presidio Officers' Club; open year-round daily 9am–5pm; closed Jan 1, Thanksgiving Day & Dec 25; 415-561-4323).* Here you'll find museum displays on Presidio history, along with maps, walking-tour brochures and helpful park personnel.

Mexicans acquired it from the Spanish in 1821. The US gained control of the Presidio in 1846, and four years later President Millard Fillmore issued an executive order to restore and expand the complex.

Montgomery Street Barracks, The Presidio

Will Elder, NPS

MUST SEE

Main Post, The Presidio

Anne Marie Scott/MICHELIN

As a US military installation, the Presidio protected California's silver and gold from Confederate troops during the Civil War and housed soldiers engaged in conflicts with western Indian tribes.

After the devastating earthquake and fire of 1906, the fort's troops helped maintain order under martial law.

In 1962 the site was named a National Historic Landmark District. The Presidio's military career finally ended in 1994, when the fort was adopted by the National Park Service. Today the Presidio Trust, an official unit of the Golden Gate National Recreation Area (GGNRA), manages the Presidio with the goal of being completely self-sufficient by 2013.

Main Post★★

Heart of the Presidio, the Main Post is home to the fort's visitor center (see sidebar p 60) and a cornucopia of other sites and activities. Pershing Square, the former home site of General John "Black Jack" Pershing, anchors the southern end of the Parade Grounds. Nearby, a monument flanked by two 17C bronze cannons marks the location of the original Presidio compound.

Officers' Row★

One block east of the Parade Grounds, Funston Street was reserved for officers' housing. The Neoclassical and Italianate cottages on the row date from 1862 and 1863.

San Francisco National Military Cemetery★
Entrance off Sheridan St. at Lincoln Blvd. Since 1884, all US veterans have had the option of being buried in the Presidio's 28-acre burial ground. Animal lovers will be moved by the nearby Pet Cemetery, where headstones

---

Crissy Field

Once a soggy marsh, Crissy Field was filled in for the 1915 **Panama-Pacific International Exposition** (*p 45*), then paved four years later with 70 acres of asphalt as an Army aircraft test site. Today the area has come full circle, restored to its natural state as a tidal marsh, beach and dune environment. Strollers, picnickers, joggers and kite fliers share the broad, flat field with sailboarders, who on fine days raise their bright sails offshore on the wind-whipped waves.

HISTORIC SITES

Fort Mason Center

mark the graves of generations of beloved Presidio pets.

Coastal Defense Batteries★

From 1853 to 1910, a number of batteries were built between Fort Point and Baker Beach to protect San Francisco Bay from invasion by sea. Today they offer **spectacular views★★★** of the sea, the Marin Headlands, and the Golden Gate Bridge. To enjoy the view, hike along the Bay Trail (see box below) through the Presidio.

Baker Beach★

Bowley St., off Lincoln Ave. at the southwest corner of the Presidio. The smooth sands and high protective dunes of Baker Beach attract two types of beachgoers. The southern end, near the parking lot, draws families; the northern end, with its more dramatic view of the Golden Gate Bridge, is popular with nude sunbathers.

Fort Mason Center★

West of Fisherman's Wharf. Entrance on Marina Blvd. at Buchanan St. 415-345-7400. www.fortmason.org.

On first glance, you might never think to stop at this complex of former military barracks, warehouses and docks. But look closer and you'll find myriad theaters, small museums, galleries, restaurants, and more than 40 non-profit organizations here. Built on a landfill during the early 20C, Fort Mason was the official embarkation point for American

---

San Francisco Bay Trail

If you walk up to Fort Mason from the Fisherman's Wharf area, you'll notice cyclists and walkers following a path that hugs the shoreline behind the Maritime Museum. This is part of the Bay Trail, which when complete will surround the Bay Area with 400mi of jogging and biking paths. For now, only 290mi of the trail exist, but that should be more than enough to give you some exercise. From Fort Mason, you can follow the trail to the Golden Gate Bridge and walk across the bright orange span for some fantastic views of the city and the Marin Headlands. *For more information: www.baytrail.abag.ca.gov.*

troops and supplies being sent to the Pacific in World War II and the Korean conflict.

During World War II alone, more than 1.5 million GIs and more than 23 million tons of cargo shipped from the fort's three docks.

The fort was decommissioned for civilian use in 1962, and the center was later transformed into a cultural complex for the community.

Today this National Historic Landmark forms part of the Golden Gate National Recreation Area and serves as a fine example of a military facility that has been converted to peacetime use. More than 15,000 events are held here each year, ranging from folk art, music, and wine festivals to trade shows, dance performances and poetry readings.

Fort Mason Museums
See Museums.

Magic Theatre
At Fort Mason Center.
See Performing Arts.

Fort Point in the Movies

The fort has been a backdrop for more movies than you'd ever guess. Here's a sampling:

Dark Passage (1947)
Vertigo (1958)
Point Blank (1967)
High Anxiety (1977)
Star Trek IV: The Voyage Home (1986)
The Presidio (1988)
Nine Months (1995)
When a Man Loves a Woman (1996)
Bicentennial Man (1999)

Greens Restaurant
At Fort Mason Center. Vegetarian cuisine with bay views. *See Restaurants.*

Fort Point National Historic Site★

Long Ave. & Marine Dr. Take Hwy. 101 North towards the Golden Gate Bridge, stay in the right lane and take the last San Francisco exit. Go through the parking lot to your right and turn left at Lincoln Blvd.

Courtesy Bridge and Tunnel Club

Fort Point and Golden Gate Bridge

St. Francis Fountain

2801 24th Street, at York Street. Open Mon-Sat 8am-10pm, Sun 8amp-9pm. 415-826-4200. stfrancisfountainsf.com. When you're in the Mission District, take a trip back in time with a visit to the city's only surviving **soda fountain**. Built in 1918, St. Francis Fountain recently reopened under new owners who are fixing the place up to look like it did in the good old days. Grab a stool at the counter and, if you dare, order a banana split royale. A heaping five scoops of ice cream with two toppings, whipped cream and, of course, a banana, this is one treat best shared with a friend.

Continue to Long Ave., which dead-ends at the fort. 415-556-1693. www.nps.gov/fopo. Open year-round Fri–Sun 10am–5pm,Closed Mon–Thu and Jan 1, Thanksgiving Day & Dec 25.

When he first designed the Golden Gate Bridge, engineer Joseph Strauss planned to sink the southern anchorage at Fort Point, but after visiting the fort he was so impressed with its Civil War-era masonry that he decided to preserve it instead. Today Fort Point seems a lonely site, standing as it does beneath a massive steel arch of the bridge.

The fort was initially designed in 1861 as a simple rectangular granite structure, but was later modified to a full-scale brick fortress with defensive towers on the east and west. Fearing Confederate attack, soldiers rushed to occupy the fort before it was even finished. By the late 1800s, however, the development of faster, more powerful rifled cannons made this and other brick forts obsolete. The last cannon at Fort Point was removed in 1886. From 1933 to 1937, the site served as base of operations for the construction of the Golden Gate Bridge. The National Park Service restored and rebuilt Fort Point in

the 1970s, and the fort now offers visitors a taste of late-19C military life on the California coast.

Exhibits – Three floors of displays range from the fort's history to the construction of the Golden Gate Bridge. Exhibits in the various soldiers' quarters depict life at Fort Point during the Civil War days.

Demonstrations, Tours & Videos – Check listing at the Sallyport for daily programs. Watch how soldiers loaded a Napoleon 12-pounder field cannon during the Civil War or take a 30-minute guided tour. There are also videos documenting the fort's history and the construction of the Golden Gate Bridge.

Mission Dolores★

16th & Dolores Sts. 415-621-8203. www.missiondolores.org. Open May–Oct daily 9am–4:30pm. Rest of the year daily 9am–4pm. Closed Jan 1, Easter Sunday, Thanksgiving Day & Dec 25. Suggested donation: $5.

"Dolores" means sorrow, and missing this lovely—and integral—piece of San Francisco's history would be sad indeed.

The sixth mission in the Alta California chain, Mission Dolores was founded in 1776 near the

Mission Dolores

present-day corner of Camp and Albion streets, two blocks east of its present site. Officially the Mission San Francisco de Asis, Mission Dolores is so-called for a nearby lake named after Our Lady of Sorrows.

Interior of the chapel, Mission Dolores

The present chapel was completed in 1791, though illness among the neophytes (Native Americans who were newly converted to Christianity) impeded the mission's growth. By the time the mission was secularized in 1834, the neophytes had all but abandoned it. During the Gold Rush days, the area surrounding the mission became a haven for vice. The Catholic church reacquired the property in 1860 and enlarged the complex to accommodate its growing congregation. The present **church★** (1918) achieved basilica status in 1952.

Chapel★★

This remarkably sturdy structure, with its 4ft-thick stucco walls, survived major earthquakes in 1868, 1906 and 1989. It is the oldest intact building in San Francisco, and thanks to a 1995 restoration program, it now appears as it did in 1791

Cemetery★

On the south side of the mission, you'll find this tranquil cemetery, where many of the city's early leaders, including Luis Antonio Arguello, the first governor of California under Mexican rule, and Francisco De Haro, San Francisco's first mayor, are buried.
You'll recognize their names on streets nearby.

Octagon House★

2645 Gough St. at Union St. 415-441-7512. www.nscda.org/museums/california.htm. Open Feb–Dec 2nd & 4th Thu & 2nd Sun noon–3pm. Closed Jan & major holidays.

These days many people use feng shui to create harmony and balance in their homes. In the 1860s, people built octagonal houses to improve their health. At the time, it was thought that this unusual floor plan allowed for more light and ventilation than that of an ordinary square-cornered house. Judge for yourself at the Colonial Dames Octagon House in Cow Hollow. Built in 1861, the house now serves as an art museum. The house, which has a view of the Golden Gate from its cupola, was built only a few years after the Gold Rush and was a family home until the 1920s.

The curious architecture is worth a trip in itself, but once inside you can admire the Colonial Dame's collection of early-American furniture, portraits, samplers, pewter and ceramics.

History buffs will appreciate the room devoted to America's Founding Fathers; here, you'll find a collection of signatures and handwritten documents by all but two of the 56 signers of the Declaration of Independence.

Octagon House

MUST SEE

Courtesy Bridge and Tunnel Club

Public Playground: The Sutro Baths

Millionaire Adolph Sutro's most beloved contribution to San Francisco was the Sutro Baths, a public swimming facility. Five cents paid for transportation to the pools on any one of three private railroads; a dime paid for admission to the complex; and for a mere quarter, visitors could swim. The freshwater pool and six saltwater pools—ranging in temperature from bathwater-warm to ocean-water-cold—were engineering marvels. Holding more than 1.5 million gallons of seawater, they could be filled or emptied by the tides in an hour.Despite their popularity, the Sutro Baths were not commercially successful. Partly transformed into an ice-skating rink in 1937, the baths were eventually destroyed by fire, and the Golden Gate National Recreation Area incorporated the ruins in 1980.

Sutro Bath Ruins★

Access by foot off 1090 Point Lobos Ave. 415-239-2366. www.nps.gov/goga/clho.htm www.sutrobaths.com

Sutro Baths – The raw, exposed ruins of Sutro Baths no longer evoke the grandeur they once represented. A gargantuan public swimming complex adjacent to **Cliff House★** (*see For Fun*), the baths cost an estimated $1,000,000 to build in 1896. The complex was the brainchild of Prussian-born engineer and one time mayor of San Francisco, Adolph Sutro, who struck it rich in Nevada's Comstock silver lode.

Totalling seven different swimming pools, the original baths allowed water to flow in from the sea at high tide.The baths survived in various incarnations since their original foundation, but after their demolition in the 1960s only concrete structures remain. Lupine and ice plants now cover the hills surrounding the baths' concrete foundation, and a tunnel once used to dump the dirt that collected in the baths pierces the bluff to the north. Follow the path above the tunnel to an overlook, where you can watch the waves crash off the rocky cliffs. Sea birds still bathe at the site but the water is brackish, the pools small.

PARKS

When you begin to feel trapped by the city's concrete jungle, take a break at one of San Francisco's many parks and gardens. With its splendid location bordered by the ocean and bay, San Francisco claims some truly great areas for recreation. Oh, and be sure to wear a flower in your hair.

🌿 Golden Gate Park★★★

Bounded by Great Hwy. & Fulton St. and Lincoln Way & Stanyan St. 415-831-2700. http://sfrecpark.org/ggp.aspx.

If you're old enough to remember the "Summer of Love" in 1967, Golden Gate Park probably brings to mind images of masses of tie-dyed-T-shirt-clad hippies and throbbing rock concerts in Speedway Meadow.
A bit more low-key today, the 1,017-acre park now provides a place for residents and visitors—some 13 million visitors each year—to escape the harried pace of the city.
Planning for Golden Gate Park began in the 1860s, when a land dispute with Mexico and fears that San Franciscans would eventually be overcrowded spurred city leaders to plan a park that would rival New York City's Central Park, already under construction. William Hammond Hall oversaw the daunting task of converting the sandy plot into a lush recreational area. When he retired, John McLaren took over as park superintendent; under his care, the area blossomed into Golden Gate Park as we know it today.

Recreation – The largest urban park in the US, Golden Gate offers 27mi of paths, 7.5mi of equestrian trails and provides fields for a wide variety of games, including baseball, tennis, golf and even pétanque.

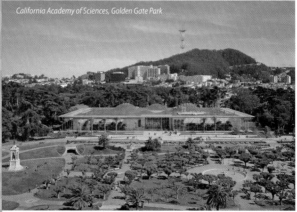

California Academy of Sciences, Golden Gate Park

Tips for Visiting Golden Gate Park

Stop for maps and information at the **Beach Chalet** visitor center *(415-751-2766; open year-round daily 9am–6pm)* or **McLaren Lodge** *(415-831-2700; open year-round Mon-Fri 8am–5pm)*. John F. Kennedy Dr. *(north)* and Martin Luther King, Jr. Dr. *(south)* form the park's two main thoroughfares. JFK Drive *(between Kezar Dr. & 19th Ave.)* closes to vehicular traffic Sundays and most holidays. On Saturdays, Middle Drive West closes south of the Polo field *(between 19th Ave. & MLK, Jr. Dr.)*. Parking is available throughout the park; disabled-parking spaces are located in the Music Concourse.

California Academy of Sciences★★

55 Concourse Dr. Open year-round Mon–Sat 9:30am–5pm, Sun 11am–5pm. Closed Thanksgiving Day, Dec 25. Adult $29.95. 415-379-8000. www.calacademy.org.

Encompassing an aquarium, a planetarium, a natural history museum, and a 4-story rainforest, San Francisco's venerable museum of natural history and science reopened in 2008 in a ground-breaking new structure designed by Pritzker Prize–winning architect Renzo Piano. Central among its "green" features is a 2.5-acre living roof. *See Museums.*

Japanese Tea Garden

Jack Hollingsworth/SFCVB

Japanese Tea Garden★★

50 Hagiwara Tea Garden Dr. Open daily Mar–Oct 9am–6pm, Nov–Feb 9am–4:45pm. Adult $7; free Mon, Wed and Fri before 10am. http:// japaneseteagardensf.com.

If you need a meditative spot to relax after a long day of sightseeing, head to the serene Japanese Tea Garden. Here you can wander through five acres of meandering paths lined with azaleas, bonsai trees and rock gardens, and when you're ready, take a tea break at the open-air teahouse. If you're in town in

mid-March through April, be sure to see the spectacular display of cherry blossoms that paint the garden in pastel pink.

de Young Memorial Museum★★

50 Hagiwara Tea Garden Drive at John F. Kennedy Dr. 415-750-3600; deyoung.famsf.org. Open year-round Tue–Sun 9:30am–5:15pm, and Friday mid-Jan–Nov until 8:45pm. Closed Jan 1, Thanksgiving and Dec 25. Adults $10; free first

PARKS

San Francisco Shakespeare Festival

What's more lovely than a summer's day? Spending a fall afternoon watching Shakespeare in the Park! For some 20 years, the San Francisco Shakespeare Festival has been producing the Bard's works in San Francisco parks (as well as locations in other Bay area cities). Change phone number to 415-558-0888. giving more than 50,000 people the opportunity to see a professional play free of charge. If you visit San Francisco between July and October, come see what all the ado is about. *For information: 415-865-4434 or www.sfshakes.org.*

Tuesday of every month. Admission tickets to the de Young include same-day admission to the Legion of Honor.

Badly damaged in the 1989 Loma Prieta earthquake, the original museum has been replaced by a daring building (Herzog & de Meuron) that opened in 2005. A major force on the West Coast museum scene, the de Young specializes in American fine and decorative art from the pre-Columbian era to the present. It also has significant holding in African art, Oceanic art, and textiles. See Museums.

Conservatory of Flowers

Carol Simowitz/SFCVB

San Francisco Botanical Garden at Strybing Arboretum★★

9th Ave. at Lincoln Way. 415-661-1316. www.sfbotanicalgarden.org. Daily Apr–Oct 9am–6pm, Nov–Mar 10am–5pm. Adult $7; free 2nd Tue of every month.

With 8,000 species of plants from all over the world represented in its 55 acres, the San Francisco Botanical Garden is a must-see for any nature enthusiast.

San Francisco's Mediterranean climate enables the arboretum to nurture plants from all over the world, including some that no longer grow in their native habitats. Walk through the Cloud Forest, where special mist machines supplement the San Francisco fog, wander the Redwood Nature Trail, or visit the Primitive Plant Garden, filled with cycads and horsetail ferns. *Free guided walks are offered daily at 1:30pm.*

Conservatory of Flowers★

100 John F. Kennedy Dr. at Conservatory Dr. 415-831-2090. www.conservatoryofflowers. org. Open year-round Tue–Sun 10am–4:30pm (last entry at 4pm). Adult $7; free first Tues of every month.

Colorful exhibits here are not only a joy to see, they teach visitors about current conservation efforts to save tropical habitats worldwide. Highlights include the steamy lowland tropics, home to the conservatory's most valuable plants; aquatic plants, where giant water lilies grow up to 5ft in diameter; and the lovely collection of orchids in highland tropics.

Children's Playground and Carrousel
See For Kids.

Golden Gate National Recreation Area★★

Headquarters at Fort Mason, Bldg. 201, McArthur St. 415-561-3003. www.nps.gov/goga. Headquarters open year-round Mon–Fri 9am–5pm.

Embracing San Francisco's northern and western boundaries as well as Angel Island, Alcatraz, and a large portion of coastal Marin County, the 80,000-acre Golden Gate National Recreation Area is more than twice the size of San Francisco. Established by an act of Congress in 1972, the park system came about largely through the efforts of US Congressman Phillip Burton, who championed the movement to preserve the area's unused military lands as parks for nature conservation and recreation. Today some 15,000 visitors visit the GGNRA each year to explore the 700 historic landmarks, miles of trails, redwood forests, beaches, and undeveloped coastal lands. The umbrella of the GGRNA covers a total of 37 different sites; whether you discover history, explore arts and culture, indulge

Golden Gate Bridge from China Beach, Golden Gate National Recreation Area

Peter Wrenn/MICHELIN

in adventure or simply drink in natural beauty, you'll be sure to leave enriched by the experience. Those listed below are described in this guide:

PARKS

Yerba Buena Gardens★★

Mission St. between Third & Fourth
Sts., South of Market.
See Neighborhoods.

Neighborhood Parks

Alta Plaza Park

Bounded by Jackson, Scott, Clay &
Steiner Sts., Pacific Heights.
At the heart of the exclusive
Pacific Heights neighborhood,
Alta Plaza Park offers a great view
of San Francisco's distinctive
architecture, along with
basketball and tennis courts
and a children's playground. On
the south side of the park, five
staircases connect the U-shaped
terraces John McLaren built to
soften the hill's vertical slope.
Today they provide excellent
views of the city. Across from
the terraces lie a famous series
of elaborate Italianate Victorian
houses at 2637–2673 Clay Street.

Buena Vista Park

Entrance at Haight & Baker Sts.,
Haight-Ashbury.
San Francisco's oldest park
offers a glimpse of nature amid
the counterculture of Haight-
Ashbury. John McLaren, who
was instrumental in landscaping
both the Golden Gate and the
Alta Plaza parks, had a hand in
planning this one, too, in the
early 1900s. If you're willing to
brave the steep hill, you'll be
rewarded with spectacular views
of San Francisco's residential areas
sweeping off to the blue waters of
the bay. Avoid this park at night.

Lafayette Park

Bound by Washington, Laguna,
Gough & Sacramento Sts.,
Pacific Heights.
A four-block oasis with beautiful
landscaping, Lafayette Park is a
wonderful place to walk your dog
or to stop for a picnic on a warm
day. The park offers a number
of walking paths as well as two
tennis courts and a fenced-in
playground. The northern edge of
the park faces historic **Spreckels
Mansion★★** (see Neighborhoods),
currently owned by novelist
Danielle Steel.

Dolores Park

Bound by 18th, Dolores, 20th and
Church Sts., Mission District
On the border of the Mission
and Castro districts, lush, hilly
Dolores Park was laid out in 1905
and served as a cemetery for two
Jewish temples. Today it is a very
popular neighborhood gathering
place for local residents of all
stripes—from twenty-something
hipsters to picnicking families to
shirtless sunbathing men.

Dolores Park

©Daniella Nowitz/Apa Publications

Huntington Park
Bound by California, Taylor, Sacramento and Mason Sts., Nob Hill.
Banked slightly above street, Huntington Park gracefully crowns Nob Hill. John McLaren, who designed Golden Gate Park and other Bay Area public gardens, oversaw the design and cultivation of this 1.75-acre plot, donated to the city after Collis Huntington's opulent mansion on the adjacent lot (where Grace Cathedral now stands) was destroyed in the 1906 fire. Blackwood acacias and sycamores thrive here, framing the 20C replica of Rome's Tartarughe ("Tortoise") Fountain that forms the park's centerpiece. Purchased in Italy by William Crocker's wife to beautify the family estate, this replica was moved here in 1955.

Ina Coolbrith Park
Taylor and Vallejo Streets.
Dedicated to California's first poet laureate, this steep series of steps and terraces (also known as the Vallejo Steps) climbs up the eastern flank of Russian Hill to afford great views of the Bay Bridge and North Beach, as well a peek of Alcatraz to the north.

Portsmouth Square
Bounded by Clay, Kearny & Washington Sts., Chinatown.
See Neighborhoods.

Washington Square Park
Bound by Columbus Ave and Union, Stockton, Filbert and Powell Sts.
With a broad, sunny lawn and clusters of willow, cypress and sycamore trees, this pentagonal park occupies the heart of North Beach. The popular neighborhood gathering spot was donated to the city by its first mayor, John W. Geary, and set aside as a public park in 1847 by Jasper O'Farrell, surveyor of San Francisco's downtown street grid. After Columbus Avenue sliced off its southwest corner in 1873, the park was landscaped to Victorian taste with shade trees and a broad, curving path for promenading. Today, elderly Asians gather each morning to practice t'ai chi; come afternoon, visitors and locals alike picnic on the grassy lawn.

Yerba Buena Gardens
Bordered by Mission, Folsom, 3rd and 4th Sts.
In addition to hosting galleries and kid-friendly activities, Yerba Buena Gardens is a delightful outdoor oasis in the heart of the South of Market neighborhood, full of landscaped lawns, fountains (including a waterfall memorial to Dr Martin Luther King, Jr), and countless benches for relaxing.

Lincoln Park

Encompassing some 100 acres of the city's northwestern corner, Lincoln Park is home to the Palace of the Legion of Honor (*see Museums*), an 18-hole golf course, and the Western Terminus of the Lincoln Highway. Conceived in 1913, the Lincoln Highway was the United States' first coast-to-coast road. A replica of the Western Terminus Marker now stands in front of the Legion of Honor.

PARKS

View from Twin Peaks

Mount Davidson Park

Between Myra Way, Dalewood Way and Juanita Way.

Mount Davidson Park encompasses the upper portion of Mount Davidson, the city's highest natural point. Originally called Blue Mountain, the 929ft peak was renamed in 1911 in honor of George Davidson, a charter member of the Sierra Club. Today, the crest is home to a 103ft concrete cross, erected in 1934, where sunrise services are held every Easter. Not looking for a hike? You can also see the cross cameo in the film *Dirty Harry* (1971).

Twin Peaks★★★

From Haight St. drive south on Clayton St. to Carmel St.; cross and continue up Twin Peaks Blvd. to Christmas Tree Point on the left.

These two high points dominate the horizon west of downtown and are visible from more areas of the city than Mt. Davidson, highest point in San Francisco at 929ft. The two distinct but adjacent peaks reach 904ft (north peak) and 908ft (south peak). Architect Bernard Maybeck, who designed the Palace of Fine Arts for the 1915 Panama-Pacific Exhibition, had grandiose plans for Twin Peaks, including a great monument at the summit with waterfalls cascading to the valley below. Most visitors content themselves with the grand panorama of the north and east sides of the city from the parking lot at Christmas Tree Point, although it is possible to climb up the grassy slopes of either peak for a view to the west as well. On clear days, Mt. Diablo to the east in Contra Costa County, and Mt. Tamalpais, to the north in Marin County, come into view.

Fort Funston

Enter from Rte. 35 (Skyline Blvd.) just south of John Muir Dr. 415-561-4323.

This expansive former military post overlooking the Pacific Ocean was established in 1898 during the Spanish-American War but never tested in combat. The fort was renamed in 1917 in honor of General Frederick

Funston, the Presidio co-commandant who organized military forces to maintain order in San Francisco in the aftermath of the 1906 earthquake and fire. With the approach of World War II, heavy cannonry was installed; Battery Richmond Davis, built in 1938, held two 16in guns. In a strategy worthy of Lewis Carroll, destination-less "roads" were created within Funston's grounds at this time to confound any invaders arriving by sea.

Today the former military lands (decommissioned in 1963) are managed by the GGNRA as a 250-acre park. Ice plants cloak the dunes atop bluffs that rise 200ft above a clean sand beach; these dunes are considered among the finest hanggliding spots in the US. Visitors gather on a viewing deck to watch the aerialists in flight. The north end of the park is a stopover for migratory Central and South American bank swallows, which burrow into the bluffs and nest there from April through July. At that time, the habitat is closed to public visitation. The scenic Sunset Trail (.75mi) meanders atop the windswept dunes and past

Battery Davis before looping back to the parking lot. More ambitious hikers may link this trail to other sections of the Coastal Trail for a 4.7mi walk to the Cliff House.

Sigmund Stern Memorial Grove

19th Ave. and Sloat Blvd.
www.sterngrove.org.

Presented to the city as a park in 1931 by Rosalie Stern in memory of her husband Sigmund, this 33-acre sylvan "grove" lies at the bottom of an east-west-running ravine. Redwoods and fragrant eucalyptus trees hem the sides of the narrow valley surrounding Stage Meadow, which forms a natural amphitheater.

Free musical performances are staged as part of a popular, long-running concert series endowed by Mrs. Stern in 1938. Music lovers of every stripe bring blankets and picnic fare to enjoy concerts in a range of musical styles from jazz to opera. Just east of Stage Meadow sits the dignified, Victorian Trocadero (1892), built by earlier landowner George M. Greene and popular as a saloon before Prohibition.

Fort Funston

PARKS

WALKING TOURS

✎ Walking Tour: North Beach

Nestled between Fisherman's Wharf and the steep slopes of Russian Hill and Telegraph Hills, North Beach is best known for its Italian roots, Beatnik history, and lively nightlife scene. Originally a beach, the area was landfilled and industrialised in the 19C, also becoming home to the infamous Barbary Coast red-light district.

◗ *Begin on Columbus Ave. at Jack Kerouac Alley, between Broadway and Pacific Ave.*

City Lights Bookstore

261 Columbus Ave. Open year-round daily 10am–midnight. Closed Thanksgiving Day and Dec. 25. 415-362-8193. www.citylights.com. Founded in 1953 by poet Lawrence Ferlinghetti, this former beatnik hangout was the first all-paperback bookstore in America. It remains one of the best-known independent shops in the US.

Vesuvio Café

255 Columbus Ave. 415-362-3370. vesuvio.com Across Jack Kerouac Alley from City Lights, Vesuvio is another

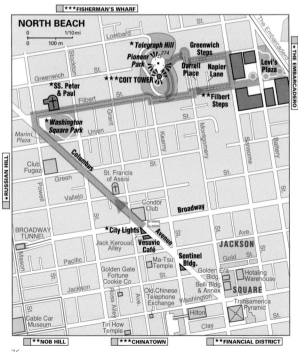

landmark of North Beach's Beat heyday. It was here that a black-clad crowd of beatniks gathered on October 13, 1955, before attending Ginsberg's now legendary reading of "Howl" at the Six Gallery (long gone from its former Marina District location).

Sentinel Building
916 Kearny St.

Glance down Columbus Ave. toward the Financial District for an impressive view of the **Transamerica Pyramid** *(See Landmarks).*

The Sentinel Building, a green, copper-trimmed, flatiron-shaped office building (1905, Salfield and Kohberg) rises in the foreground. Filmmaker Francis Ford Coppola purchased and restored the tower in the 1970s; on the ground floor, **Café Zoetrope** *(415-291-1700)* maintains a light menu and wine from Napa Valley's Neibaum-Coppola estate.

❍ *Walk north on Columbus Ave. to Broadway.*

Broadway
Broadway between Columbus Ave. & Montgomery St.

Though its reputation for danger, vice and sin has gentled in recent decades, the strip of topless clubs and sex shops along Broadway harks back to San Francisco's less-than-savory past.

Broadway's notoriety originated in the waterfront dives of Sydney Town in the 1850s, when a zone of dance halls, brothels, gambling dens and outlaw nests known as the Barbary Coast arose along lower Pacific Avenue, extending

to present-day Jackson Square and parts of Chinatown. Sailors on shore leave enjoyed the strip's diversions at great peril: "Shanghaiing" was an all-too-common practice (the word, meaning "recruiting someone forcefully for maritime service," is said to have originated here). Civic pressure led to the cleanup of the Barbary Coast after the 1906 earthquake and fire, and bars offering exotic entertainment were restricted to Broadway, where they have persisted, mostly undisturbed, for years. Several risqué venues opened in the 1960s and early 1970s, among them the Condor Club at the intersection of Broadway, Columbus and Grant Avenues. For several decades a neon figure of "queen of topless dancing" Carol Doda hung provocatively above the street, drawing scores of visitors.

❍ *Continue walking north on Columbus Ave.*

Columbus Avenue

Designed in 1972 as a direct path from the Financial District to the industrial zone growing along the northern waterfront, this broad, busy avenue traces the valley between Russian and Telegraph Hills, indiscriminately cutting across the city's square grid and creating several confusing six-way intersections. Called Montgomery Avenue at its construction, it was later renamed for Christopher Columbus to honor North Beach's Italian community. The blocks between Broadway and Filbert Street, lined with bakeries, trattorias, delicatessens and cafes, preserve the neighborhood's Italian soul.

Washington Square Park
Bounded by Columbus Ave, Powell St. Union St. See Parks.

◖ *Cross Washington Square Park.*

Saints Peter and Paul Church
666 Filbert St., north side of Washington Sq. Open year-round Mon–Fri 7am–4pm, weekends 6.30am–7pm. 415421-0809.
Built in Gothic Revival style with Italianate details, this handsome, twin-spired church (1924) reflects North Beach's multi-ethnic character, offering Mass in English, Italian, and Cantonese. The imposing façade bears the opening line of Dante's *Paradiso*, and the interior is warm and inviting, enclosed by an unusual flat ceiling of dark wood and illuminated by banks of votive candles and richly colored stained glass windows. A spectacular 40ft-high altar, made of Mediterranean marble and onyx, features a sculpted reproduction of da Vinci's *Last Supper*.

◖ *From the church, walk east of Filbert St. and climb the hill, following the "Stairs to Coit Tower" signs. To avoid the very steep climb, take the 39-Coit bus from Washington Square (bus stop is the corner of Union & Stockton Streets).*

Telegraph Hill
The abrupt 274ft rise that punctuates the eastern edge of North Beach was named for a long-vanished semaphore (a precursor to modern telegraph systems) erected atop its summit in 1849. Gold Rush-era shacks and tent cities that dotted the steep, rocky flanks developed into working-class neighborhoods that persisted until the early 20C, when the automobile opened the way for wealthier citizens. Most of the structures on the hill (and in surrounding North Beach) burned to the ground during the 1906 fire. At the hill's summit, panoramic views encompass major landmarks including the Golden Gate Bridge, Twin Peaks, Lombard Street, Alcatraz, and the Bay Bridge.

Coit Tower
Summit of Telegraph Hill. See Neighborhoods.

◖ *From Coit Tower, descend the curving sidewalk along Telegraph Hill Ave. to the first corner and turn left at Filbert St.*

Filbert Street Steps
Coit Tower to Sansome Street. See Landmarks.

◖◖ Walking Tour: Haight-Ashbury

Although more than three decades have passed since the Human Be-In and Summer of Love, a countercultural ethos still clings to Haight-Ashbury, usually called "the Haight." Named for two streets intersecting at its heart, this neighborhood draws hordes of young people to its thrift stores, bars and cafes. With 90 percent of its housing stock predating

Speaking Walls: The Murals of San Francisco

San Francisco tallies nearly 600 wall paintings within its 49sq mi. Some record traditional history. Others serve as vibrant pictorial voices for communities without expression in mainstream art institutions—groups united by race, ethnicity, class, gender or politics. The great Mexican muralist **Diego Rivera** visited the city during the early 1930s, executing important works at the San Francisco Art Institute and the Pacific Exchange. Fresco murals at Coit Tower and the Beach Chalet reflect Rivera's influence during this period.

During the late 1960s, **David Alfaro Siqueiros** improved techniques for outdoor painting, and the Mission District witnessed an explosion of outdoor art the following decade. The fences, walls and garage doors of Balmy Alley, off 24th Street, were originally decorated by schoolchildren. Many Mission District artists painted their first murals in the alley, including **Patricia Rodríguez, Graciela Carillo** and **Irene Pérez**, who later founded **Mujeres Muralistas**, a group of women artists who pictured the beauty of their cultures. Many of those early murals were subsequently replaced in the 1980s by the PLACA group—this time with themes of the struggle for peace in Central America. More recent Balmy Alley murals include portraits of Mexican art icons, a relief mural made with plywood cut-outs, and a mural tribute to Mujeres Muralistas. Maradiaga Mini-Park contains murals drawn to teach local kids about their Latin-American heritage.

Following is a brief list of some exceptionally interesting Mission District murals. For more information, drop by or call the **Precita Eyes Mural Arts and Visitors Center** *(2981 24th St. near Harrison St.; 415-285-2287; www.precitaeyes.org)* which offers lectures and walking tours of Mission District murals as well as a useful map pinpointing more than 90 murals in the area if you wish to explore the neighborhood independently.

- *Las Lechugueras* (1983) by Juana Alicia; Taquería San Francisco, 24th and York Streets.
- *Silent Language of the Soul* (1990) by Juana Alicia and Susan Cervantes; Cesar Chavez Elementary School, Shotwell & 22nd Sts.
- *Five Hundred Years of Resistance* (1993) by Isaías Mata; St. Peter's Church, 24th St. at Florida St.
- *Maestrapeace* (1995) by various women artists; Women's Building, 3543 18th St.

1922, the Haight also boasts some of the city's loveliest Victorian homes.

◗ *Begin at Haight and Stanyan Streets, walking east away from Golden Gate Park.*

Haight Street

Lined with coffee shops, boutiques, pubs and restaurants, Haight Street from Stanyan Street to Central Avenue is the neighborhood's main drag. The narrow sidewalks are often packed with skateboarders, shoppers and tourists; incense wafts from New Age shops; and rock music pulses from frenetic thrift stores. Pop into **Amoeba Records** *(1885 Haight St., 415-831-1200)* located in a converted bowling alley, to peruse diverse music offerings including

WALKING TOURS

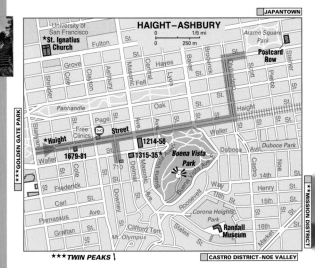

experimental rock, hip-hop, electronica and jazz.

A block further, **The Alembic** (*1725 Haight St., 415-666-0822*) serves up some of the most creative cocktails in the city (*See Nightlife*).

While the buildings here are not the district's most distinguished, some, like the colorful, curvaceous structure at no. 1679–81 (1904, James F. Dunn), display a certain charm. Nearby, you'll pass San Francisco's only

> **Take a Break**
>
> For a break from walking, enjoy tapas and sangria at **Cha Cha Cha** (*1801 Haight St., 415-386-7670, www.cha3.com*), artisan ales and upscale pub fare at **Magnolia Gastropub and Brewery** (*1398 Haight St., 415-864-7468, www.magnoliapub.com*) or organic wood-fired cuisine at **Nopa** (*560 Divisadero, 415-864-8643, www.nopasf.com*).

worker-owned theater, the funky **Red Vic Movie House** (*1727 Haight*). Here you can watch cult classics, documentaries, and indie favorites from comfy couches while noshing on organic treats.

❍ *Turn right at the intersection of Haight and Ashbury Streets and walk up Ashbury 1 ½ blocks.*

Grateful Dead House
710 Ashbury Street.

The Haight blossomed into a countercultural lodestar in the late 1960s, drawing hippies from around the US with promises of mind-altering drugs and free love. In 1967, Jerry Garcia's Grateful Dead held court at 710 Ashbury Street (now a private home); neighbors included Janis Joplin and members of Jefferson Airplane. These musicians invented the wandering, melodic "San Francisco Sound" that catapulted them to international fame. Haight-Ashbury reached

MUST SEE

its peak later that year during what became known as the Summer of Love, when some 75,000 young people flocked to the neighborhood, sleeping in Golden Gate Park and attending free concerts and parties.

◐ *Walk back on Ashbury to Waller Street; turn right. At Masonic Avenue, turn left.*

1315–1335 Waller Street and 1214–1256 Masonic Avenue

Hundreds of unique, eye-catching Victorian period houses, most in the Queen Anne style, adorn Haight-Ashbury. Characterized by asymmetrical massing, a panoply of external surfaces and designs, bay windows and sometimes turrets, the homes date primarily from the building boom of the 1880s and 90s. Because houses in the Haight were so much in demand, Queen Annes were frequently built in rows of four or five similar structures, but a variety of color and detailing options provided ample opportunity for homeowners to distinguish their abodes from their neighbors'. Many fanciful examples of Queen Annes in the neighborhood were restored during the gentrification trend that swept the neighborhood in the 1980s and 90s.

The rows at 1214–1256 Masonic Avenue and 1315–1335 Central Avenue embody the spirit of the style.

◐ *Continue on Masonic Ave to Haight Street. Turn right on Haight Street.*

Bound Together Anarchist Collective Bookstore
1369 Haight St. Open daily 11.30am–7.30pm. 415-431-8355. boundtogetherbooks. wordpress.com.

For decades this volunteer-run outlet has supplied required reading for the counterculture: books, magazines and pamphlets on alternative thinking and the remaking of society.

◐ *Continue east on Haight Street.*

Buena Vista Park

Rising abruptly south of Haight Street, between Central Avenue and Baker Street, this sylvan hill boasts tantalizing glimpses of the city from between the trees that crowd its steep slopes. The 36.5-acre park was reserved for public use in 1867, and John McLaren supervised the planting of cypress, live oak, pine and eucalyptus trees during the early 1900s. Sweeping views of San Francisco's residential areas stretch away toward bay and ocean from the summit, reached after a challenging climb.

◐ *To explore the grittier Lower Haight neighborhood, continue on Haight Street past Divisadero. Or, to reach Alamo Square, continue to Divisadero and turn left. Walk five blocks north on Divisadero to Hayes and turn right. Alamo Square is one block away.*

Alamo Square

Bordered by Fulton, Scott, Hayes and Steiner Sts.

This green-lawned square is famous for its **"Postcard Row" view★★★** of Financial District skyscrapers rising above virtually identical, restored Victorians at 710–720 Steiner St., between Hayes and Grove Streets. The houses also featured in the opening scenes of the Full House TV show. *See Landmarks.*

Walking Tour: Mission District

With its dual identity as the city's Latino enclave and its hub for young hipsters, the Mission District is one of the city's liveliest neighborhoods. It's also one of its warmest—a high ridge on the scenic western edge of the district protects the area against the chill fogs and ocean winds that afflict many other parts of the city.

Begin at the intersection of 16th and Dolores Streets.

Mission Dolores
3321 16th St. at Dolores St. Open daily 9am–4pm. Closed Jan 1, Thanksgiving Day, Dec 25. Donation requested. 415-621-8203. http://missiondolores.org.
San Francisco's oldest extant structure was dedicated in 1776, marking the official founding of the city. In 1791 a new chapel was built; it was renovated and reconsecrated as a parish church in 1859. Restored in 1995, the **chapel★★** retains the original tile roof and bells. A **cemetery★** holds the remains of, among others, the first Mexican *alcalde* (mayor) of Yerba Buena. *See Landmarks.*

Walk south on Dolores Street towards 17th Street.

Dolores Street
Rolling hills, lofty palm trees and an eye-catching assemblage of architectural styles characterize this attractive stretch of Dolores Street. At 18th Street, Mission Dolores' architecture is echoed in the huge, red-tile-roofed Mission High School (1926, John Reid, Jr.).

Dolores Park
Bordered by 18th, 19th, Dolores and Church Sts.
Lush, hilly Dolores Park *(See Parks)* was laid out in 1905 and served as a cemetery for two Jewish temples. South of the park is **Liberty Street** *(between 20th and 21st Sts.),* lined with Victorians dating from the 1860s. All major styles are represented, including Italianate (no. 109), Stick (nos. 111–121), and Queen Anne (no. 123).

Turn left at 18th Street, and right at Valencia Street.

Valencia Street
Between 16th and 23rd Street.
A magnet for the young and the hip, this section of Valencia Street and the cross streets to Guerrero Street have been transformed into a trendy "new Bohemia", lined with a profusion of restaurants, cafes, thrift shops, bookstores and bars. At 826 Valencia is a literary nonprofit founded by Dave Eggers that doubles as a pirate store. The area east of Valencia and south of 16th Street today remains predominantly Latino and largely working class, though artist and entrepreneurs have discovered the Mission, giving rise to a thriving bar scene.

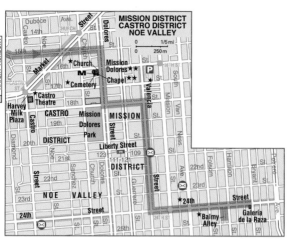

○ From Valencia Street, turn left at 24th Street.

24th Street
Between Mission & Potrero Sts.
This lively, tree-lined shopping strip exudes the gritty, exuberant aura of the Mission District. Community residents flock here daily to pick up produce, meats, cheeses and baked goods. Bright awnings shade fruit stands overflowing with exotic picks; Spanish rolls off the tongues of shopkeepers and shoppers alike; and modest eateries serve up Latin American treats.

○ From 24th Street, turn right on Balmy Alley.

Balmy Alley
Between Treat and Harrison St.
Stroll down Balmy Alley to admire colorful murals adorning nearly every garage door and wall surface.

Galeria de la Raza
2857 24th St. at Bryant St.; open Wed–Sat noon–6pm; 415-826-8009 www.galeriadelaraza.org.
Occupying an unassuming corner storefront, Galeria de la Raza has sustained and nurtured the Chicano art movement since 1970. The gallery showcases new artists along with established ones; exhibits reflect Chicano and Latino social and cultural issues.

✿⁀Walking Tour: Golden Gate Park

Encompassing more than 1,017 acres of meadows, gardens and public buildings, verdant Golden Gate Park is the largest cultivated urban park in the US. Stretching from Haight-Ashbury to the Pacific, it has 27 miles of footpaths and 7.5 miles of equestrian trails, all linking an enchantingly natural, yet entirely man-made, landscape of lakes, swales and

WALKING TOURS

Dutch Windmill, Golden Gate Park

Phillip H. Coblentz/SFCVB

woods. *See Parks and Museums* for additional information on many of the attractions listed here.

○ Enter the park at 9th Ave. and Lincoln Way, onto Martin Luther King Jr. Dr. On the left is the San Francisco Botanical Garden.

San Francisco Botanical Garden at Strybing Arboretum
415-661-1316.
www.sfbotanicalgarden.org.
This outstanding botanical collection comprises 8,000 species of plants from all over the world. The arboretum emphasizes regions of Mediterranean climate, with collections from California, the Cape Province of South Africa, southwestern Australia and Chile. Other attractions include a hillside garden of succulents; the Cloud Forests, where mist emitters supplement the fog; the Nature Trail; and the Primitive Plant Garden of moss,

cycads, horsetails, gingko trees, ferns, and conifers. The Garden of Fragrances features a wall built of stones removed from a medieval Spanish monastery purchased by William Randolph Hearst.

○ Continue on Martin Luther King Jr. Drive. Past its intersection with Middle Drive East, turn right to follow the signs for the Shakespeare Garden.

Shakespeare Garden★
Martin Luther King, Jr., Dr. and Middle Dr. E.
Established in 1928, this small English garden nurtures plants mentioned in the works of William Shakespeare. The locked box in the back wall contains a bust of the Bard, a copy from the sculpted image at the poet's tomb carved by Gerard Johnson after Shakespeare's death in 1616.

○ Return to Martin Luther King Jr. Drive and continue north. For Stow Lake, continue until Stow Lake Drive and turn right. Otherwise, turn right onto Hagiwara Tea Garden Drive.

Stow Lake★
Stow Lake Dr.; access from John F. Kennedy Dr. or Martin Luther King, Jr., Dr. Boathouse open daily 10am–4pm, weather permitting.
www.parks.sfgov.org.
The park's main irrigation reservoir surrounding Strawberry Hill is the largest of the 15 man-made lakes that dot Golden Gate Park. Swarms of waterfowl share the water with the small boats which may be rented on the northwest shore. The

MUST SEE

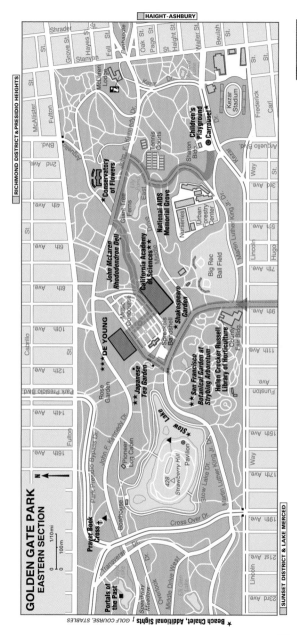

GOLDEN GATE PARK
EASTERN SECTION

N

1/10mi
100m

Shrader St.
Hayes St.
Grove St.
Stanyan St.
Fell St.
Oak St.
Page St.
Haight St.
Waller St.
Beulah St.
Frederick St.
Carl St.

McAllister St.
Fulton St.
Arguello Blvd
2nd Ave
4th Ave
6th Ave
8th Ave
10th Ave
12th Ave
14th Ave
16th Ave
Park Presidio Blvd
Cabrillo St.
Fulton St.

McLaren Lodge
Kezar Dr.
Kezar Stadium

John F. Kennedy Dr.

★ Conservatory of Flowers

Tennis Courts
Sharon Bldg.
★ Children's Playground
Carrousel ★

Giant Tree Ferns

National AIDS Memorial Grove

Nurseries
Urban Forestry Center

John McLaren Rhododendron Dell

★★ California Academy of Sciences ★★

Music Concourse

★★★ DE YOUNG

Spreckels Bandshell

★ Shakespeare Garden

Big Rec Ball Field

Rose Garden

★★ Japanese Tea Garden

Helen Crocker Russell Library of Horticulture

County Fair Bldg.

★★ San Francisco Botanical Garden at Strybing Arboretum

Stow Lake

Strawberry Hill
428
Pavilion

Prayer Book Cross ★ †

Pioneer Log Cabin

Boathouse

John F. Kennedy Dr.
Park Presidio Bypass Dr.

Cross Over Dr.

Portals of the Past ■

Transverse Dr.

Speedway Meadow

Overlook
Middle Drive West

Elk Glen Lake

Lincoln Way
21st Ave
23rd Ave
19th Ave
17th Ave
15th Ave
11th Ave
9th Ave
7th Ave
5th Ave
3rd Ave

Martin Luther King Jr. Dr.
Lincoln Way
Hugo St.
Way
Funston Ave.
Ave.

Middle Dr. E

★ Beach Chalet, Additional Sights / GOLF COURSE, STABLES

WALKING TOURS

85

Stow Lake

© Rafael Ramirez Lee/Bigstockphoto.com

428ft summit of Strawberry Hill, reached by footpath, is the highest point in the park. Constructed in 1894, a waterfall named for industrialist Collis P. Huntington cascades 125ft from the summit to the surface of the lake.

❍ *Once on Hagiwara Tea Garden Dr., the Japanese Tea Garden will be on your left.*

Japanese Tea Garden★★
Hagiwara Tea Garden Dr. 415-666-3232; japaneseteagardensf.com. *See Parks.*
Harboring a delightful maze of winding paths, stone lanterns, ornamental ponds, bonsai, a wooden pagoda, a Zen garden and a teahouse, this tranquil, five-acre garden has been an attraction since it was built for the Midwinter Fair of 1894. The garden continued operating under the direction of master gardener Makoto Hagiwara, who also tended the tea concession and is credited with inventing the fortune cookie here in 1909.

❍ *Continue on Hagiwara Tea Garden Dr.*

de Young Museum
50 Hagiwara Tea Garden Dr. 415-750-3600. www.famsf.org/deyoung. *See Museums.*
Herzog & de Meuron, Swiss architects whose designs include London's Tate Modern, designed this new (2005) three-story structure of recycled redwood, eucalyptus and copper. The de Young is noted for its American Collection, including works by Bierstady, Eakins, Sargent, Homer, Diebenkorn, O'Keefe, Hopper and Wood. Other collections include African and Oceanic art, and pre-Columbian American art.

Park Chow
1240 9th Ave. 415-665-9912. www.chowfoodbar.com.
A half block from Golden Gate Park, this busy, friendly spot serves up healthy American comfort fare at sidewalk tables, inside by the fireplace, or up on the rooftop deck.

MUST SEE

◐ Cross the Music Concourse in front of the De Young Museum to reach the California Academy of Sciences.

California Academy of Sciences
55 Music Concourse Drive. 415-379-8000. www.calacademy.org. See Museums.

Pritzker Prize-winning architect Renzo Piano designed this 410,000sq-ft, $400 million structure, which features a "living roof" made up of 1.7 million native California plants and 60,000 photovoltaic cells. This unique lid not only helps the building meld with its surroundings but also absorbs rainwater to decrease runoff and provides natural insulation. Inside are housed the Kimball Natural History Museum, the Steinhart Aquarium and the Morrison Planetarium.

◐ Take the path just north of the Academy of Sciences (see map) to reach the John McClaren Rhododendron Dell.

John McClaren Rhododendron Dell

At the heart of this 20-acre, spring-blooming garden stands a statue of John McLaren contemplating a pinecone. The life-size proportions and quiet pose contrast with the host of heroic bronze figures that surround the nearby Music Concourse, an ironic contradiction to McLaren's lifelong campaign to keep statues from cluttering the park's scenery.

◐ At John F. Kennedy Dr., turn right.

Conservatory of Flowers★
100 John F. Kennedy Dr. at Conservatory Dr. 415-831-2090. www.conservatoryofflowers.org. See Parks.

This ornate Victorian glass greenhouse composed of two wings flanking an octagonal rotunda is Golden Gate Park's oldest structure. Originally purchased by James Lick for installation on his estate in San Joes, the greenhouse was shipped in prefabricated parts from Dublin but arrived after Lick's death in 1876. San Francisco businessmen purchased the building and donated it to the park. Seasonal blooms in formal geometric designs grace the parterres in front.

◐ Turn right on Middle Drive E., and bear left onto Bowling Green Drive. On the left is the Aids Memorial Grove. Continue on onto Bowling Green Drive to reach the Koret Children's Corner. Cross through the parking lot on the left.

Koret Children's Corner

A pioneering concept when it opened in 1888, this municipal playground was centered on the sandstone Sharon Building, which provided refreshments, stored play equipment and stabled goats for the kids' "barnyard." The magnificent **Hershell-Spillman Carrousel★**, its princely stable of carved wooden animals under a dome supported by 16 fluted columns, was built in 1912 and restored in 1984. *See Parks.*

EXCURSIONS FROM SAN FRANCISCO

Although you may be justifiably hesitant to leave San Francisco, within a two-hour drive of the city you'll find ancient stands of redwoods and windswept beaches, the intellectual hub of Berkeley and the charming sun-washed towns of Monterey and Carmel, not to mention the world-renowned Wine Country. With all this to choose from, your most difficult decision will be where to start!

EAST BAY

The dynamic university city of Berkeley has an unending appetite for political activism, energetic intellectualism and cultural diversity.
Up in the Berkeley Hills, the city boasts beautiful neighborhoods with stunning views of San Francisco. Oakland, Berkeley's neighbor to the south, boasts revitalized waterfront and civic center districts, an exceptional museum, and ambitiously restored mid-19C to 20C residential and commercial buildings.

Berkeley★★

⟳ *8mi northeast of San Francisco via I-80 over the Bay Bridge to Exit 11, and east on University Ave.; or take BART to Berkeley station.* 510-549-7040 or 800-847-4823. www.visitberkeley.com.

A small city with a big reputation for political protest, Berkeley offers much more than a dynamic community. A bustling university, a vast collection of museums, and excellent shopping and dining districts all add to the city's appeal.

University of California, Berkeley★★

One block east (uphill) from the BART Berkeley Station.
UC Berkeley, which ranks among the country's best universities in nearly all of its academic programs, is notorious for political activism and highly regarded for its scientific achievements. Visit the campus to be inspired by the proactive students and gorgeous architecture.

Walking tours of the campus depart from the visitor center *(101 Sproul Hall; 510-642-5215; www.berkeley.edu; Mon–Sat 10am, Sun 1pm).*
Along the way, you'll pass a number of landmarks, including the **Valley Life Sciences Building★**—the largest academic building in the US when it was completed in 1930. Climb up to the observation platform in the **Campanile★★** (Sather Tower) for **panoramic views★★** of the Berkeley Hills.
Depending on your interests, you may also want to visit the **UC Berkeley Art Museum★** *(2626 Bancroft Way; 510-642-0808; www.bampfa.berkeley.edu)* or the **UC Botanical Garden★** *(200 Centennial Dr.; 510-643-2755; http://botanicalgarden.berkeley.edu).*

MUST SEE

Campanile of UC Berkeley with a view to San Francisco Bay

© Rafael Ramirez/Fotolia.com

Telegraph Avenue★
Between Bancroft & Dwight Ways.
A haven for the intellectually elite and the chronically hip, this little street is packed with bookstores, art vendors, brew pubs, record stores and cafes. Stop by and soak up the culture.

Oakland★

○ *12mi east of San Francisco. Take I-80 across the San Francisco-Oakland Bay Bridge.* **Tourist** *information: 510-839-9000 or www.oaklandcvb.com.*

Just a short hop across the Bay Bridge from San Francisco, Oakland makes a great excursion for anyone in the Bay Area who wants to give their wallet a break from the high costs of the city. Kids, sports fans, and shopaholics will all find something to occupy them in this city across the Bay.

Oakland Museum of California★★
1000 Oak St. 510-238-2200. www.museumca.org. Wed–Sun 11am–5pm (Friday open until 9pm).

Closed major holidays. $12 Adults $9 seniors and students with valid ID $6 youth (9-17). Free children under 8.
Designed to explain and promote California, the Oakland Museum will introduce you to the art, history, and natural sciences unique to California. The 7.7-acre cultural complex celebrates California's diversity on all three floors of the building that *New York Times* critic Ada Louise Huxtable deemed "one of the most thoughtful revolutionary structures in the world."

Paramount Theatre★★
2025 Broadway St. 510-465-6400. paramounttheatre.com.
A striking example of Art Deco architecture, the Paramount Theatre currently serves as both a movie theater and a performing-arts center. Drop by to see either the Oakland Ballet or the Oakland East Bay Symphony perform, or, if you're a history buff, take a tour of the complex.

EXCURSIONS

USS Hornet★★

Pier 3, Alameda. ◗ *Take Atlantic Ave. north off Webster St. (Rte. 61) and follow signs. 510-521-8448. www.uss-hornet.org. Open year-round Mon–Sun 10am–5pm. Closed Jan 1, Thanksgiving Day & Dec 25. $15 Adult $12 Seniors, Students with ID $6, Military with ID $6, Youth (5-17). Free children (4 and under).*

Be sure to explore the USS *Hornet*, one of the most distinguished military ships in US history. Commissioned in 1943, this aircraft carrier served 16 consecutive months in the Pacific Campaign during World War II. After earning nine battle stars for its service in that war, the *Hornet* went on to serve in Vietnam and later to recover the astronauts of Apollo 11.

East Bay Area★

East of San Francisco. ◗ *Take I-80 East across the San Francisco-Oakland Bay Bridge.*

East of the ridgeline backdropping Berkeley and Oakland lies a series of hills and valley overshadowed by regal Mt. Diablo. Nestled among the small towns there lie a number of lesser-known, though equally significant, must-sees.

Blackhawk Museum★★

3700 Blackhawk Plaza Circle, Danville. ◗ *33mi east of San Francisco via I-680 to Sycamore Valley Blvd. exit. 925-736-2277. www.blackhawkauto.org. Open Wed–Sat 10am–5pm. $10 Adults, $7 Students (with ID) and Seniors Free children under 6.*

With more than 90 vintage automobiles on display dating from the 1890s to the 1960s, this museum will appeal to anyone who loves the feel of the open road.

Eugene O'Neill National Historic Site★★

Kuss Rd., Danville. ◗ *28mi east of San Francisco. Take I-80 East to Hwy 24; drive east on Hwy. 24 to I-680, and take I-680 south from Walnut Creek to Danville. 925-838-0249. www.nps.gov/ euon. Public visitation by advance reservation, Wed–Sun, with guided tours at 10:00am and 2pm (allow 2 hours). Closed Jan 1, Thanksgiving Day & Dec 25. Reservations required.*

If you love theater and literature, be sure to tour this site, home of Tau House, where playwright Eugene O'Neill lived and worked from 1937 to 1944. The famous playwright —who won four Pulitzer Prizes and the Nobel Prize for Literature (1936)— wrote his best-known works here, including *The Iceman Cometh* and the autobiographical *A Long Day's Journey into Night.*

John Muir National Historic Site★

4202 Alhambra Ave., Martinez. ◗ *30mi northeast of San Francisco. Follow I-80 East to Exit 24 and take Rte. 4 east; exit at Alhambra Ave. and turn left. 925-228-8860. www.nps.gov/jomu. Open year-round Wed–Sun 10am–5pm. Closed Jan 1, Thanksgiving Day & Dec 25. $3 (16+).*

Often called "The Father of our National Park System," John Muir (see box below) was one of America's first conservationists. Muir spent the last years of his life, from 1890 until his death in 1914, at this two-story Italianate home.

John Muir

Years before we dealt with the thorny political issues of pollution and development encroaching on natural areas, John Muir warned: *"If the importance of forests were at all understood, even from an economic standpoint, their preservation would call forth the most watchful attention of government."* Not only did Muir establish the **Sierra Club**, but he also played a role in the creation of the **Grand Canyon, Sequoia and Kings Canyon**, and **Mt. Rainier national parks**. Today **Muir Woods** honors the great conservationist's legacy.

Mount Diablo State Park★

North Gate Rd., Walnut Creek. ○ *35mi east of San Francisco. From Oakland, take Rte. 24 East to Walnut Creek and go east on Ygnacio Valley Rd.; turn right on Walnut Ave. 925-837-2525. www.mdia.org. Open daily 8am–dusk. $10/car.*

Ready for a hike? If you make it to the top of 3,849ft-high Mount Diablo here, you'll be rewarded with an **extensive breathtaking view★★★** that stretches as far as Mount Lassen (165mi northeast).

🍇 WINE COUNTRY★★★

Picnicking on artisan cheeses and fresh crusty bread amid acres of gnarled grapevines. Sipping wine on a terrace above a hillside of silvery olive trees. Touring caves heady with the sweet smell of fermenting grapes. This is the Wine Country.

From the renowned Napa Valley west to the Sonoma Valley and north to the Russian River Valley, Northern California's Wine Country creates a feast for the senses that would make Bacchus (the Roman god of wine) envious.

Lying inland within an hour's drive north of San Francisco, Napa Valley and Sonoma County thrive on the abundant sunshine and fertile soil that produce grapes for some of North America's finest wines. Differences in elevation, proximity to the sea and exposure to sun, fog and wind create myriad microclimates, each affected by factors as seemingly insignificant as a dip in a mountain ridge or the tilt of a slope. The first wineries were established in northern California in the late 19C. In recent decades the Wine Country has exploded into a center not only for wine, but for fine art, gastronomy and tourism.

Napa Valley★★★

○ *41mi northeast of San Francisco via I-80 East and Rte. 29 North. Sights in the Napa Valley are described from south to north.*

Cradled between two elongated mountain ranges, this world-renowned valley extends about 35mi from San Pablo Bay northwest to Mount St. Helena. Many of California's most prestigious wineries cluster along traffic-choked Route 29—the St. Helena Highway—as it passes through the towns of Napa, **Yountville★**,

EXCURSIONS

Wine Country Tour

There's seemingly no end to the wineries you can visit in **Northern California's Wine Country**, so we've provided a place to start—with wineries acclaimed for fine art exhibits, innovative architecture and historical interest, plus some purely renowned for wine. Most wineries are *open daily 10am–5pm. Call for tasting fees and reservations.*

Artesa Vineyards and Winery – *1345 Henry Rd., Napa. 707- 224-1668. www.artesawinery.com.* In 1872 the Codorníu family of Barcelona became Spain's first producers of sparkling wine made in the méthode Champenoise tradition. Their Napa Valley operation occupies an innovative contemporary structure (1991, Domingo Triay), with galleries holding 16C–17C European winemaking equipment.

The Hess Collection Winery – *4411 Redwood Rd., Napa. 707-255-1144. www.hesscollection.com.* Nestled on the slope of Mt. Veeder, this beautifully renovated structure contains one of the nation's largest and finest private art collections open to the public, as well as a state-of- the-art winemaking facility.

Domaine Chandon – *1 California Dr., Yountville. 707-944-2280. www.chandon.com.* The free guided tour of this winery, commissioned by the owners of France's famed Moët et Chandon, explains the principal stages of sparkling-wine production according to the traditional méthode Champenoise.

Robert Mondavi Winery – *7801 St. Helena Hwy. (Rte. 29), Oakville. 888-766-6328 www.robertmondaviwinery.com.* This striking building (1966) heralded a new generation of modern wineries designed to showcase art and architecture as well as wine. Sculptor Beniamino Bufano's figure of St. Francis greets visitors beneath an arched entry.

Beringer Vineyards – *2000 Main St. (Hwy. 29), St. Helena. 707-963-7115. www.beringer.com.* The centerpiece of Napa Valley's oldest continuously operating winery, established in 1876 by German immigrants Jacob and Frederick Beringer, is the 17-room Rhine House (1883).

Rombauer – *3522 Silverado Trail North, St. Helena. 800-622-2206, www.rombauer.com.* A cozy tasting room, great views of the valley and exceptional wines all contribute to this hillside winery's enduring popularity.

Castello di Amorosa – *4045 N. St. Helena Highway, Calistoga. 707-967-6272. www.castellodiamorosa.com.* This reproduction of a medieval Tuscan castle— complete with drawbridge, secret passageways, and watch tower—offers Italian-style wines and horse-drawn vineyard tours.

Schramsberg – *1400 Schramsberg Rd. Calistoga. 800-877-3623. www.schramberg.com.* A must-visit for sparkling wine fans, Schramsberg offers tours of 120-year-old caves and tastings of its acclaimed sparkling wines.

Sterling Vineyards – *1111 Dunaweal Lane, Calistoga. Off Rte. 29. 707-942-3344. www.sterlingvineyards.com.* From the parking area, an aerial tramway transports you up to Sterling's winery, which perches atop a 300ft knoll overlooking the Napa Valley.

Peter Wrenn/MICHELIN

Oakville, Rutherford, **St. Helena**★ and **Calistoga**★. Others dot the more tranquil **Silverado Trail**★, which parallels Route 29 to the east.

di Rosa Preserve★★

5200 Carneros Hwy. ○ Rte. 121 (2.5mi west of Rte. 12). Visit by guided tour only; reservations required. Call for tour times: 707-226-5991. www.dirosapreserve. org. $12 (free admission the 1st & 3rd Wed of each month).

The two-and-a-half-hour guided tour of this 1886 stone winery showcases the art collection of René di Rosa, son of a US ambassador to Italy who came to San Francisco from Yale University in the 1950s as a young newspaper reporter. In 1960 he purchased 460 acres of abandoned vineyards in the Carneros area of lower Napa Valley, converting the winery into his home.

Over four decades he amassed a huge personal collection produced in the greater San Francisco area in the last half of the 20C; the collection now includes 2,000 works in all media.

Napa Valley Museum★

55 Presidents Circle, Yountville. www.napavalleymuseum.org. Open year-round Wed–Mon 10am–5pm. Closed Tue, Jan 1, Thanksgiving Day & Dec 25.

Mud Baths and Mineral Springs

Volcanic activity in the northern Napa Valley has erupted in a multitude of geysers and hot springs, many of which have been harnessed to fuel the famed spas of **Calistoga**★. Founded in 1859, this resort hamlet hunkers in the shadow of Mount St. Helena (4,343ft) where tourists flocked—both then and now—to experience the health-promoting power of the local waters. Today you can get an hour-long basic mud-bath package, including mud bath, herbal wrap and mineral whirlpool bath, for $50 to $70; massages, facials and mineral-pool soaks will cost you extra. The Calistoga Chamber of Commerce *(1458 Lincoln Ave., Calistoga; 707-942-6333; www.calistogachamber.com)* can provide a list of spas in the area. Here are some places to start:

Calistoga Spa Hot Springs –
1006 Washington St. 707-942-6269. www.calistogaspa.com.

Calistoga Village Inn and Spa –
1880 Lincoln Ave. 707-942-0991. www.greatspa.com.

Dr. Wilkinson's Hot Springs Resort – *1507 Lincoln Ave. 707-942-4102. www.drwilkinson.com.*

Golden Haven Spa & Resort –
1713 Lake St. 707-942-6793. www.goldenhaven.com.

Mount View Hotel & Spa –
1457 Lincoln Ave. 707-942-6877. www.mountviewspa.com.

Tips for Visiting Wine Country

Go in spring when the mustard plants turn the vineyards yellow, or in fall—the more crowded season—to see the harvest. Complete lists of wineries and their hours are available from the visitors' bureaus in **Napa Valley, Sonoma Valley and Russian River Valley**. Most wineries offer tours and tastings (most charge a tasting fee). Some offer tours by appointment only, so call before you go. Contact the following agencies for information:

Napa Valley Conference & Visitors Bureau – *1310 Napa Town Center, Napa. 707-226-7459. www.napavalley.com.*

Sonoma Valley Visitors Bureau – *453 1st St. E., Sonoma. 707-996-1090. www.sonomavalley.com.*

Sonoma County Tourism Information – *59 4th Street, Santa Rosa. 707-577-8674. sonomacounty.com.*

Russian River Valley Chamber of Commerce & Visitor Center *16209 1st St., Guerneville. 707-869-3533. www.russianriver.com.*

Russian River Wine Roads – *800-723-6336. www.wineroad.com.*

Recreation

Napa Valley Wine Train – *(707-253-2111 or 800-427-4124. www.winetrain.com)* takes passengers on a 3-hour, 36mi tour of the Wine Country from Napa to St. Helena. Relax aboard vintage 1910 train cars as you ride through breathtaking scenery.

Photo by Up & Away Ballooning
Sonoma County Tourism Bureau

Ballooning – Up, up and away! If you want to see the **Wine Country** from above, consider a balloon tour: **Above the Wine Country** *(707-829-9850; www.balloontours.com)*, **Adventures Aloft** *(707-944-4408 or 800-944-4408; www.nvaloft.com)*, **Aerostat Adventures** *(707-433-3777; www.aerostatadventures.com)*, and **Bonaventura Balloon Company** *(707-944-2822 or 800-359-6272; www.bonaventureballoons.com)*.

Biking is a great way to enjoy the **Wine Country. Wine Country Bikes** *(707-545-7960; www.winecountrybikes.com)* and Get-Away Adventures *(707-763-3040; www.getawayadventures.com)* provide rentals and tours through the area.

707-944-0500. $5 Adults $3.50 Seniors $2.50 Youth (under 17)

Dedicated to promoting Napa Valley's cultural and environmental heritage, this museum features changing exhibits ranging from fine arts to history to natural sciences, as well as the permanent exhibit Land and People of the Napa Valley.

MUST SEE

Sonoma Valley★★

○ *The town of Sonoma is 49mi north of San Francisco via US-101 north to Rte. 37 East to Rte. 121/12.*

Enjoying a reputation for excellent produce and other farm products, as well as for wines, Sonoma County incorporates the diverse viticultural areas of the Sonoma Valley, the Russian River Valley, the Dry Creek Valley and the Alexander Valley. In the southern portion of the county, the historic town of Sonoma dominates the **Sonoma Valley★★**, which parallels Napa Valley on the west side of the Mayacamas Mountains.
In the northern end of Sonoma County, the **Russian River Valley★** follows the curving path of its namesake river as it meanders south through the town of **Healdsburg★** and veers west to the coast. Known for its Zinfandel wines, the delightful **Dry Creek Valley★** extends from Lake Sonoma to just south of Healdsburg; the neighboring **Alexander Valley★** centers along Route 128 northeast of Healdsburg *(tourist information: Healdsburg Area Chamber of Commerce: 217 Healdsburg Ave.; 707-433-6935; www.healdsburg.org).*

Sonoma★★

Site of California's northernmost and final mission, this charming community is the Wine Country's most historically significant town. It was born as the site of the San Francisco Solano Mission (below) in 1823 and retains its historic flavor, even though many of its venerable adobe buildings are now occupied by shops, restaurants and inns.

Lake Sonoma Overlook
11mi north of Healdsburg via Dry Creek Rd. Follow signs from Lake Sonoma visitor center.
It's worth a drive up to this outlook for great **views★★** of the hilly area surrounding the sapphire waters of **Lake Sonoma★.**

Sonoma's eight-acre central plaza★ *(bounded by Spain St., Napa St. & 1st Sts. W. & E.)* was the scene, on June 14, 1846, of the Bear Flag Revolt, an uprising of American settlers desirous of US control of California. Hoisting a white flag emblazoned with a brown bear and a star, the group proclaimed California an independent republic. The following month, American forces captured Monterey, declared California a US possession, and effectively ended the short-lived republic. Near the plaza's northeast corner, a bronze statue of a soldier raising the Bear Flag commemorates the revolt.

Sonoma State Historic Park★★
Sites open year-round daily 10am–5pm. Closed Jan 1, Thanksgiving Day & Dec 25. $2 for all sights (tickets available at any of the three park sights below). www.parks.ca.gov.
Around the plaza stand an array of buildings now open to the public under the auspices of the state historic park.
Across First Street from the plaza, **San Francisco Solano Mission★** *(corner of E. Spain St. & 1st St. E.; 707-938-9560)* was established in 1823 by Padre José Altamira to help solidify Mexican holdings

Mustard growing between rows of old vine zinfandel in Kenwood, Sonoma Valley

Sonoma County Tourism Bureau

against invasion. All that remains of the mission complex are the restored chapel and part of the priests' quarters.

Overlooking the plaza, the two-story adobe **Sonoma Barracks**★ was built in 1841 *(across 1st St. E. from the mission; 707-939-9420)*. The barracks once housed Mexican troops who guarded the new pueblo; today it contains artifacts from the various periods of Mexican and American settlement. Nearby, the final home of General Mariano Vallejo (1807–1890) was named **Lachryma Montis**★, or "tear of the mountain" in Latin, for the mountain spring on the property *(W. Spain St. near 3rd St. E.; 707-938-9559)*. Vallejo was called by Mexican governor Figueroa to oversee the secularization of the Sonoma mission and the founding of a defense outpost there. Appointed commander of all Mexican troops in California in 1835, Vallejo was elected to California's first state senate in 1850. His home's airy interior paints a delightful picture of the general's genteel lifestyle.

Jack London State Historic Park★★

◗ *10mi northwest of Sonoma at 2400 London Ranch Rd., Glen Ellen. Open year-round daily 10am–5pm. Closed Jan 1, Thanksgiving Day & Dec 25. $8/car. 707-938-5216. www.jacklondonpark.com.*

Sprawling among peaceful hills in the shadow of Sonoma Mountain, 800-acre "Beauty Ranch" was home to author Jack London (1876–1916) and his second wife, Charmain. In 1911 the couple began construction of a four-story mansion of lava boulders and

Jack London State Historic Park

Courtesy Bridge and Tunnel Club

Sonoma Valley Wine Tour

Viansa Winery – *25200 Arnold Drive, Sonoma, 707-935-4726. www.viansa.com.* Perched on a hilltop at the entrance to Sonoma Valley, this Tuscan-inspired winery and marketplace offers great views and picnic areas.

Buena Vista Winery – *18000 Old Winery Rd., Sonoma. 707-938-1266. www.buenavistawinery.com.* Buena Vista was founded in 1857 by Hungarian immigrant Agoston Haraszthy, who was the first to experiment with European varietals in Northern California. The lovely stone Press House dates back to 1862.

Chateau St. John – *8555 Sonoma Highway, Kenwood. 707-833-4134. www.chateaustjean.com.* A stunning property with beautiful gardens, a sunny patio, green lawns for picnicking, and a tasting room offering Chardonnay, Cabernet Sauvignon, Merlot and Gewurztraminer.

Benziger Family Winery – *1883 London Ranch Rd., Glen Ellen. 707-935-3000. www.benziger.com.* The tram tour of this sustainable winery takes visitors out into the vineyard to learn how the grapes are grown without using pesticides.

redwood logs that they dubbed Wolf House. In August 1913—just days before they were to move in—a fire roared through the house, leaving only the stone shell. Devasted, the Londons never rebuilt. They lived instead in a modest cottage on the ranch, where Jack died at age 40. Trails lead past the ruins of **Wolf House★** and the cottage where the man who penned such classic adventure stories as *The Call of the Wild, Sea Wolf and White Fang* lived and worked.

Petaluma Adobe State Historic Park★★

◑ *10mi west of Sonoma at 3325 Adobe Rd. Open year-round daily 10am–5pm. Closed Jan 1, Thanksgiving Day & Dec 25. $2. 707-762-4871. www.parks.ca.gov.*

Mexican commander Mariano Vallejo chose this hilltop overlooking the rolling Sonoma County countryside as the site of his headquarters in 1834. Here he established a 100sq mi ranch on

the land grant he received from the Mexican government. Rancho Petaluma thrived until Vallejo leased the property in September 1850. Today the restored two-story structure, half its initial size, re-creates the atmosphere of a prosperous ranch with authentic period pieces.

Don Clausen Fish Hatchery★★

3333 Skaggs Springs Rd. ◑ *11mi north of Healdsburg. Open daily 9:30am–4:30pm (closed Tue & Wed in winter). 707-433-9483. www.parks.sonoma.net./laktrls.*

Located behind the visitor center at **Lake Sonoma★**, this state-of-the-art hatchery building was created by the Army Corps of Engineers to lessen the environmental damage to Dry Creek when the dam was built. Here you can watch the spawning and hatching activities of steelhead trout, and coho and chinook salmon *(viewing times: Jan–Mar for steelhead trout; early Oct–Dec for salmon).*

EXCURSIONS

Bixby Creek Bridge, Big Sur

CENTRAL COAST

Big Sur★★★

Isolated redwood canyons, green meadows and sheer grantic ridges plunging into the frothy sea define this dramatic coastline at the western edge of the continent. Big Sur's history, mystique and spectacular scenery make it one of California's most popular tourist destinations.

◗ *Hwy. 1 between Carmel and San Simeon. 831-667-2100.*

This rugged coastline, extending 90mi south from Carmel, is celebrated for its charismatic, wild beauty. A precipitous coastal wall, plunging 4,000ft to the sea, thwarted settlement by the Spanish, who called it El País Grande del Sur—"the Big Country to the south." Mid-19C homesteaders trickled into narrow valleys to ranch and log redwoods.

Completion of the highway in 1937 opened the area to visitors. Traveling south from Carmel, the concrete-arch **Bixby Creek Bridge,** build in 1932, is one of the 10 highest single-span bridges in the world.

Point Sur State Historic Park preserves an 1889 stone lighthouse built 272ft above the surf on a volcanic rock connected to the mainland by a sandbar.

Near the **village of Big Sur** (23mi south of Carmel), in the forested Big Sur River valley, **Andrew Molera State Park** and **Pfeiffer Big Sur State Park** offer coastal vistas and access. Four miles south, the venerable **Nepenthe★** bar and restaurant boasts sweeping views from its cliffside terraces 800ft above the ocean.

Hearst Castle ★★

◗ *Rte. 1, 98mi south of Monterey. Visit by reservation only. 805-927-2020. www.hearstcastle.org.*

MUST SEE

Overlooking the Pacific Ocean from atop a Santa Lucia Mountain crest, this 127-acre estate and the opulent mansion crowning it embody the flamboyance of William Randolph Hearst.

It was eclectically designed and lavishly embellished with the newsman's world-class collection of Mediterranean art.

Hearst's father, George, purchased this ranch in 1865. In 1919, William hired architect Julia Morgan to create a "bungalow" that over 28 years grew from a modest residence to "The Enchanted Hill." Morgan designed a Mediterranean Revival-style main house and three guest houses.

From twin Spanish Colonial towers with arabesque grillwork and Belgian carillon bells, to Etruscan colonnades that complement the Greco-Roman temple façade of the **Neptune Pool**★, and gold-inlaid Venetian glass tiles of the indoor **Roman Pool**★, the design emerged as a mélange that defies categorization.

The 65,000sq-ft main house contains 115 rooms, including 38 bedrooms, 41 bathrooms, two libraries, a billiards room, beauty salon and theater. All feature Hearst's art holdings, including silver, 16C tapestries, terra-cotta sculpture and ancient Greek vases that line the shelves of a 5000-volume library.

Five different tours are offered, all lasting 2hrs and departing form a visitor center at the foot of the hill. Shuttle buses climb 10min to the castle, with spectacular views en route. As they wait, visitors may take in a 40min film.

Carmel★★

One of California's most picturesque villages is Carmel-by-the-Sea (as it is officially named). A charming square mile of carefully tended houses under a canopy of pine, oak and cypress, Carmel has long attracted artists, writers, celebrities and tourists.

The village was originally planned in the 1880s as a seaside resort for Catholics. By the turn of the 19C that venture had failed, and Frank Devendorf, a young real-estate speculator from San Jose, had begun planning a community that would preserve the pristine beauty of the natural setting and attract "people of aesthetic taste."

In 1905, aspiring poet George Sterling settled in Carmel and enticed fellow writers and artists to the area. Soon the quaint village developed a reputation as a bohemian retreat, with Sterling hosting abalone parties for literary figures Jack London, Mary Austin and Upton Sinclair. Among celebrated residents of Carmel in later decades were photographers Edward Weston and Ansel Adams, writer Lincoln Steffens and poet Robinson Jeffers.

Carmel's charming cottages and village ambience are protected by a strict 1929 zoning ordinance concerning commercial development.

Upscale boutiques, galleries, inns and restaurants are concentrated in the commercial area *(Ocean, 6th & 7th Aves. between Junipero Ave. & Monte Verde St.).*

Scenic Road winds south along the beachfront for 1.5mi, ending at Carmel River State Beach *(accessible off Ocean Ave.; one-way southbound for first 0.7mi).*

San Carlos Borroméo de Carmelo Mission★★★

3080 Rio Rd. at Lasuen Dr. Open year-round Mon–Sat 9.30am –5pm, Sun 10.30am–5pm. Closed Easter Sun & Mon, Thanksgiving Day, Dec 24–26. $6.50 Adults, $4 Seniors, $2 Children, Free under 6. 831-624-1271. www.carmelmission.org.

Headquarters of the California mission chain during its expansive early years, the Carmel mission was founded by Padre Junípero Serra, whose remains are interred here. The old chapel (now designated a basilica) and rebuilt mission grounds continue to serve as an active parish church and school.

In 1771, when Padre Serra decided to move the mission out of the presidio at Monterey, he chose this site near the Carmel River. The current stone church was completed in 1797, replacing an adobe chapel built in 1782. The mission began a slow decline in 1803 when the headquarters was transferred elsewhere. In 1931 a 50-year preservation effort restored the complex. Built of rough-hewn sandstone, the façade is offset by two asymmetrical, Moorish-style bell towers and a star window. The interior is supported by catenary arches that slope upward more steeply than a traditional barrel vault.

Below the elaborate **reredos** lies the grave of Padre Serra. The mission's original stone baptismal font remains in the baptistry.

Historical artifacts and liturgical art are displayed throughout the church and in several small mission museums.

Carmel City Beach★★

Heavy surf; swimming not recommended.

This wide sweep of white sand is pounded by the breakers of Carmel Bay. Sea otters may be spotted and gray whales seen during the migratory season (Dec–Apr).

Tor House★★

26304 Ocean View Ave., ⟳ 1.2mi south of Ocean Ave. Visit by guided tour (1hr) only, year-round Fri & Sat on the hour 10am–3pm. Closed Jan 1, Dec 25. $10 Adults, $5 Students. Reservations required. 831-624-1813. www.torhouse.org.

This stone complex was built on the "tor," or rock promontory, by poet Robinson Jeffers, whose writing was inspired by the raw beauty of the Pacific coast off Carmel Point. Jeffers built the whimsical **Hawk Tower** himself; it contains his desk and chair.

Monterey★★

⟳ 115mi south of San Francisco. Follow US-101 south to Rte. 156 west to Hwy. 1 South. Visitor information: 1-877-Monterey; www.montereyinfo.org.

Once capital of California and later of sardines, Monterey mixes its Spanish colonial past with modern appeal. Bookworms come here to pay homage to John Steinbeck at **Cannery Row★** and to Robert Louis Stevenson at the **Stevenson House★** *(530 Houston St.; 831-649-7118).* Even if literature doesn't appeal to you, the city is a delight,

Monterey Bay Aquarium entrance on Cannery Row

Monterey Bay Aquarium/Rick Brown

featuring a world-class aquarium, a large collection of historical sites, and fabulous shops.

Path of History Walking Tour – This tour is a great way to visit Monterey's historic sites. **Monterey State Historic Park** *(831-649-7118; www.parks.ca.gov)* maintains many of the adobes along the route and offers guided walking tours throughout the year.

Monterey Bay Aquarium★★
886 Cannery Row. 831-648-4800. www.mbayaq.org. 10am–6pm Winter: 10am–5pm Summer/ holidays: 9:30am–6pm Summer weekends: 9:30am–8pm. $29.95 Adult, $27.95 Student (13-17, College ID) and Senior, $19.95 Child (3-12), Free Children under 3.
If you're wondering what denizens lurk beneath the waters of Monterey Bay, you've come to the right place—more than 35,000 animals and plants representing 550 species swim and sway here. Housed in a converted cannery, the aquarium is designed to incorporate the sea as an architectural element. You'll understand how when you look through the 56ft-long window into

The Outer Bay★★, an open-ocean tank that holds a million gallons of seawater. Whether you go alone to see one of the world's largest jellyfish galleries or take the kids to the hands-on **Splash Zone**★, you're sure to enjoy this award-winning aquarium.

Big Basin Redwoods State Park

⟳ *23mi northwest of Santa Cruz, take Hwy. 9 to Rte 236/Big Basin Way. www.bigbasin.org.*

Established in 1902, California's oldest state park is home to 18,000 acres of old growth and recovering redwood forest in the Santa Cruz Mountains. Visitors come for camping, backpacking, mountain biking, and of course, hiking—over 80 miles of trails traverse lush canyon bottoms and chaparral-covered slopes, passing numerous waterfalls. The easy **Redwood Loop** Trail (.5mi) showcases the tallest measured tree in the park and the two trees with the widest circumferences, while more difficult trails like the historic **Sequoia Trail** (3.5-5.5mi) encompass meadowland, creeks

and waterfalls, in addition to old growth redwoods.
Current trail maps available from park headquarters *(21600 Big Basin Way)*.

NORTH COAST

A region of fog-draped redwood forests, vertical cliffs plunging steeply into the roiling Pacific and reminders of California's logging industry, the northwestern corner of the state is appealing in its remoteness. The area immediately north of San Francisco offers a gentler landscape of pretty coastal villages, charming state parks and thriving vineyards and wineries.

Marin County★★

Marin County combines the sophisticated charm of Sausalito and the ancient redwoods of Muir Woods with the rugged seascapes of Point Reyes and the Marin Headlands. While some 240,000 suburbanites reside in this county, most settlement is on the eastern side of Mt. Tamalpais, leaving the coastal precincts in a largely natural state.

For thousands of years, the Marin area was home to the Coast Miwok Indians. Its first European visitor was purportedly Francis Drake, who set out from England in 1577 to reconnoiter Spanish defenses in the New World, but the British did not pursue their claim to the land and it became a Spanish colony. Mexicans grazed cattle here after they threw off the Spanish yoke in 1821; Americans logged the redwood forests nearly to depletion into the early 20C. During World War II, defenses were built along the Marin Headlands, and the Marinship naval shipyard employed thousands of workers. By the latter half of the 20C, upscale Marin County had become synonymous with the California lifestyle.

Sausalito★

○ *4mi north of San Francisco via US-101. 415-332-0505.*
www.sausalito.org.
Developed as a resort in the 1870s, this upscale residential community has winding streets, attractive hillside neighborhoods and fine views. Throngs of visitors arrive on sunny days and weekends to window-shop and relax in boutiques and restaurants along **Bridgeway Boulevard★**, the waterfront commercial district. The docklands of **Marinship** *(1mi north on Bridgeway)*, a shipbuilding

---

Sausalito Shopping

Here's a sampling of the shops and galleries unique to Sausalito:
Fingerhut Gallery – *690 Bridgeway. 415-331-7225. www.fingerhutart.com.* Here you'll find fine art (read pricey!) by the likes of masters Chagall, Matisse and Picasso. **Gene Hiller for Men** – *729 Bridgeway. 415-332-3636. www.genehiller.com.* One of California's premier men's clothiers proffers designs by Brioni and Canali, among other notables. **Petri's Gallery** – *675 Bridgeway. 415-332-2225. www.petrisgallery.com.* Petri's carries art glass from over 150 designers.

Homes line the Sausalito slopes

©Geoffrey Kuchera/iStockphoto.com

center during World War II, now shelter a houseboat community. The **Bay Model Visitor Center**★ *(2100 Bridgeway Blvd., 415-332-3871, www.spn.usace.army)* holds a two-acre hydraulic scale model of the San Francisco Bay and Delta. The US Army Corps of Engineers uses it to study the effects of dredging, shoreline development and other ecological projects.

Marinship

◐ *1mi north on Bridgeway to Marinship Way.*

Ninety-three ships were built here during World War II in 1942–45. Artists and small manufacturers occupy part of the site today. The **Bay Model Visitor Center**★ of the US Army Corps of Engineers *(2100 Bridgeway)* has a 1.5-acre hydraulic model of the San Francisco Bay, which simulates tidal flow through the estuary *(open Memorial Day–Labor Day Tue–Fri 9am–4pm, weekends 10am–5pm; rest of the year Tue–Sat 9am–4pm; 415-332-3871; www.spn.usace. army.mil/bmvc).*

Marin Headlands★★

◐ *Take Alexander Ave. exit from northbound US-101; from ramp, turn left, then bear right onto Barry Rd.*

This windswept landscape of coastal cliffs and hills at the north end of the Golden Gate Bridge forms part of the Golden Gate National Recreation Area. **Conzelman Road** provides spectacular **views**★★★ of San Francisco and the bridge. The road terminates at **Point Bonita Lighthouse**★ *(open year-round Sat–Mon 12.30pm–3.30pm; 415-331-1540; www.nps.gov/goga/ pobo.htm).* The **Marin Headlands Visitor Center**★ *(open year-round daily 9.30am–4.30pm; closed Thanksgiving Day, Dec 25; 415-331-1540; www.nps.gov/goga/marin-headlands.htm)* features displays on the headlands, and hiking trails thread the grassy slopes.

San Rafael Arcángel Mission

◐ *15mi north of San Francisco at 5th Ave. & A St., San Rafael. Take US-101 to Central San Rafael exit. Chapel open daily 6:30am-6:30pm. Closed holidays. 415-456-3016. www.saintraphael.com.*

The 20th mission of the California chain was founded in 1817 as a branch, or *asistencia*, to Mission Dolores in San Francisco. It was also used as a sanitarium for San Franciscans in failing health. The buildings were razed in 1870; the current replica dates from 1949.

Muir Woods National Monument★★★

◐ *19mi north of San Francisco. Take US-101 to Hwy. 1 (Shoreline Hwy.). Continue to Panoramic Hwy. and turn right, then left on Muir Woods Rd. Open year-round daily 8am–dusk. $5, children free. 415-388-2596. www.nps.gov/muwo.*

This 560-acre plot of coast redwoods is one of the last

Mount Tamalpais, Muir Woods National Monument

Damien/MICHELIN

Point Reyes National Seashore

⏵ 40 mi. north of San Francisco. Take US-101 north to Greenbrae Exit; turn west on Sir Francis Drake Blvd for 10mi, then north on Hwy 1 to first left at Bear Valley Road.
415-464-5100. www.nps.gov/pore.
This 102sq-mi park embraces white sand beaches, rocky headlands, windswept moors, salt marshes, lush forests and abundant wildlife. The cape is located where the Pacific Plate meets the North American Plate along an active San Andreas rift zone clearly marked by Bolinas Bay, Olema Valley and Tomales Bay.

The Bear Valley Visitor Center★ (west of Hwy 1 intersection) contains exhibits on local ecology and history. Hikers on the adjacent **Earthquake Trail★** (.6mi) can see a fence line that was shifted 16ft by the 1906 earthquake.

A 22mi drive from the visitor center is **Point Reyes Lighthouse★★**, clinging to a rocky shelf on a 600ft precipice. Equipped with a Fresnel lens imported from France in 1870, the lighthouse offers **sweeping views★★** of the Farralon Islands and of magnificent winter whale migrations.

At nearby **Chimney Rock,** elephant seals may be spotted in season (mid-Dec–Mar).

virgin redwood forests in the Bay Area. Muir Woods became a national monument in 1908 after Congressman William Kent donated land to the US government, insisting the park be named for conservationist John Muir. From the visitor center, the Main Trail *(1mi)* reaches **Cathedral Grove**, where trees as old as 1,000 years rise like spires. The return trail passes **Bohemian Grove**, site of the park's tallest tree, measuring 253ft *(tree is unmarked).*

A spur road from Hwy. 1, 3mi north of Panoramic Highway, leads to **Muir Beach Overlook**, where a platform affords **views★★** of the coast.

Park Shuttles

The **Point Reyes Peninsula** is an extremely popular place to visit during the winter whale-migration season when gray whales pass close to shore.

To relieve traffic congestion on the peninsula, park shuttle buses make the loop from Drake's Beach to the Point Reyes Lighthouse parking lot and on to Chimney Rock during peak visit times *(late Dec–mid-Apr weekends & holidays 9.30am–3pm)* $5, children free. **Purchase shuttle tickets** at the Drake's Beach Visitor Center. Note that during shuttle operation periods, Sir Francis Drake Boulevard south of South Beach Junction is closed to private vehicles.

The 12mi strip comprising **North Beach** and **South Beach** (follow Drake Blvd. southwest 4.7mi, turn right at sign) faces northwest into the strongest winds and roughest surf. 2mi east is **Drakes Beach,** framed by high chalk-white cliffs.

Mill Valley
Located 4mi north of San Francisco, this Marin County town of 13,600 nestles on the southern slopes of Mt. Tamalpais, and spreads to the western and northern shores of Richardson Bay.

Mount Tamalpais State Park★★
◑ *20mi north of San Francisco. Take US-101 to Hwy. 1 (Shoreline Hwy.). Continue to Panoramic Hwy. and turn right, following signs to the park.* **Open year-round daily 7am–dusk. Closed during high fire-risk days. $8/car. 415-388-2070. www.parks.ca.gov.**
The serpentine ascent to the 2,572ft east peak of Mt. Tamalpais (tam-ul-PIE-us) is rewarded with **views★★★** of San Francisco and

the Pacific coastline. Trails lace the mountain's flanks, drawing hikers and equestrians; the Pantoll ranger station *(junction of Pantoll Rd. and Panoramic Hwy.)* has maps and information on weather and trail conditions.

Sonoma County Coast★★

◑ *Along Hwy. 1 from Point Reyes Station north to Mendocino County. Visitor's information: 850 Hwy. 1, in Bodega Bay. 707-875-3866. www.bodegabay.com.*

Stretching 191mi from San Francisco to north of Fort Bragg, Highway 1 snakes along the rim of the southern half of California's North Coast.
Over the centuries, the Pacific's waves have carved the shale and sandstone rocks of the coastline here into vertical benches backed by craggy cliffs. It's worth a drive up at least as far north as Mendocino *(see p 106)* for spectacular views of steep, rocky walls being pummeled by the roiling Pacific surf.

Rugged Sonoma County Coastline

Robert Janover/Sonoma County Tourism Bureau

Sonoma Coast State Beaches★★

707-875-3483. www.parks.ca.gov. Open daily year-round. $8/car. Call for openings.

Rocky outcrops separate the 15 small, sandy crescents that punctuate this 16mi strip of coast from Bodega Head (65mi north of San Francisco) to just north of Jenner. Stop at the abundant turnouts along this part of Highway 1 to ogle spectacular oceanscapes, or just spend some time sunbathing or picnicking at the beaches. One of the most accessible of the Sonoma Coast beaches is **Goat Rock Beach★** at the mouth of the Russian River, where you'll have a unique view of river and ocean barely separated by a narrow spit of sand. From November to March, throngs of resident harbor seals vie with fishermen here to catch the schools of salmon that return each year to spawn. North of Jenner, it's slow going as the road becomes a series of sharply angled switchbacks winding high above the ocean.

Fort Ross State Historic Park★★

◆ *87mi north of San Francisco on Hwy. 1. 707-847-3286. www.parks.ca.gov. Grounds open Saturdays, Sundays and holidays. Visitor center open 10am–4pm. Closed Thanksgiving Day & Dec 25. $8/vehicle.*

Built high on an isolated promontory above a sheltered azure cove, Fort Ross was established in 1812 by members of the Russian-American Company, a commercial hunting and trading group that managed Russian trade and exploration in North America. The redwood fort reigned as Russia's easternmost outpost for nearly 40 years. Now owned by the state of California, it has been partially restored with an Orthodox chapel, officials' quarters and two blockhouses.

MENDOCINO★★

◆ *150mi north of San Francisco via US-101 north to Rte. 28 west, or via scenic Hwy. 1 north. Visitor information: 866-466-3636. www.visitmendocino.com.*

Seated on a foggy headland where the Big River meets the ocean, this picturesque Victorian village appears little changed from its heyday as a lumber town in the late 19C. Favoring New England-style architecture, it has a "skyline" of clapboard house with steep gabled roofs, wooden water towers, a Gothic Revival-style Presbyterian church (1868) and the false-fronted Mendocino Hotel (1878). Enveloping the town, **Mendocino Headlands State Park★★** *(707-937-5804, www.parks.ca.gov)* preserves **marvelous views★★** of fissure-riddled rocks and sea caves. The 1854 Ford House serves as the park's visitor center *(735 Main St.; 707-937-5397).*
Today Mendocino caters to tourists, who come here to spend a few peaceful days in charming B&Bs, shop in artisans' boutiques and fine-arts galleries, and revel in stunning views of **Mendocino Bay**.

Palo Alto★

An affluent college town of about 64,000, Palo Alto derives its name from the twin-trunked coast redwood under which Gaspar de Portolá camped on his 1769 expedition. Now single-trunked and timeworn, El Palo Alto, "the tall tree," still stands in a small park by the railroad tracks off Alma Avenue. It remains the official symbol of Stanford University.

Stanford University★★

Main Quadrangle on Serra St., Palo Alto. 650-723-2560. www.stanford.edu.

Railroad magnate Leland Stanford (1824-93) and his wife, Jane, established this private institution in memory of their late son. Now it is a leading academic and research center.
The campus—a creation of architect Charles Allerton Coolidge and landscape architect Frederick Law Olmsted—is noted for Romanesque buildings shaded by eucalyptus, bay and palm trees.
The historic heart of campus is the **Main Quadrangle**, a cloistered courtyard bordered by colonnaded buildings. Its **Memorial Church★★**, built in 1903 by Jane Stanford, is famed for its Byzantine-style mosaics, stained glass and 7,777-pipe organ. **Hoover Tower★** *(650-723-2053)*, a 285ft landmark campanile with a 35-bell carillon, offers views over campus from its observation deck.
Iris & B. Gerald Cantor Center for Visual Arts★ *(Lomita Dr. & Museum Way; 650-723-4177, museum.stanford.edu)* houses 20,000 pieces of ancient to contemporary sculpture, paintings and crafts from six continents.
The adjacent **Rodin Sculpture Garden★** contains 20 large-scale bronze casts by famed French sculptor Auguste Rodin.

Stanford Linear Accelerator Center

2575 Sand Hill Rd., just east of I-280, Menlo Park. Visitor center open daily Mon–Fri 9am–4pm. Guided tours (1.5hrs) available 3rd Fri of month; call or consult website for times. 650-926-2204. www.slac.stanford.edu.

Operated by the university for the U.S. Department of Energy, SLAC opened in 1961 as a research facility in particle physics. Within this 480-acre facility, which includes a 2mi-long linear accelerator, scientists probe the structure of matter on atomic and subatomic levels with x-rays and particle beams. In the small visitor center, exhibits describe such discoveries as quarks, and explore successes in biomedical and environmental research.
Also displayed is a skeletal cast of an ancient walrus-like mammal, Paleoparadoxia, found during excavation at SLAC.

NASA Ames Research Center

Moffett Field, Mountain View.
◐ From US-101, take Moffett Field exit; turn right to main gate, then left .4mi on R.T. Jones Rd. to Gate 17C. Visitor center open Tue–Fri 10am–4pm; Sat–Sun noon–4pm. Closed major holidays. 650-604-6274. www.arc.nasa.gov.

Founded in 1939 at a former naval air field as an aircraft research laboratory, this 430-acre facility has been a part of the National Aeronautics and Space Administration since 1958.
Now the hub of NASA information technologies, Ames is also the

lead NASA agency in the study of gravity, astrobiology and Mars exploration, to name but a few. The center harbors the world's largest wind tunnel and several advanced flight simulators.

The visitor center boasts the west coast's largest immersive theater. Displays showcase planetary exploration, space-suit technology and artifacts from past missions.

Filoli★★

Canada Rd., Woodside. ⊙ 13mi North of Palo Alto. 650-364-8300. www.filoli.org. Open Tue–Sat 10am–3:30pm, Sun 11am–3:30pm (last entrance at 2:30pm).

This 700-acre estate was built in 1916 for Empire Mine owner William Bourne (1857-1936). The modified **Georgian Revival mansion★★**, designed by Willis Polk, is furnished with 17-18C Irish and English furniture. Bruce Porter and Isabella Wood designed the **16-acre gardens★★★** in Italian and French style.

Some of the most interesting plants were gifts or purchases from foreign governments, disposing of display specimens after the 1915 Panama-Pacific Exposition.

Sierra Nevada

Stretching 400mi from the Cascade Range near Lassen Peak to Tehachapi Pass east of Bakersfield, the Sierra Nevada is the longest

Visiting Yosemite

Yosemite Lodging —Lodging, dining facilities, shops and other amenities are found at rustic Camp Curry, motel-style Yosemite Lodge and at the magnificent hotel **Ahwahnee★★★** *(lodging reservations at 559-253-5635, www.yosemitepark. com/Accommodations.aspx)* Perhaps the finest of all national park lodges. Outside the valley, a more modest array of park facilities exists at Crane Flat, Tuolumne Meadows, White Wolf and Wawona in summer, and at Badger Pass Ski Resort in winter

Yosemite Village —The administra-tive and commercial center of the park includes a post office, the **Ansel Adams Gallery** and a Wilderness Office where hikers obtain backcountry information and permits. The **Visitor Center** presents exhibits on geology and natural history. The **Yosemite Museum** houses a collection of native artifacts, changing art exhibits and the snug Yosemite Library. Behind the museum, a recreated Miwok village features reproductions of Ahwahneechee bark structures.

Happy Isles★ — At the mouth of the Merced River Canyon, a cluster of small islands split the roaring cataract into smaller channels. A delightful picnic spot at 4,050ft elevation, Happy Isles is the start of the often-spectacular **John Muir Trail.** Very popular is the short, steep jaunt to **Vernal Falls Bridge★** (.7mi); from here, the Mist Trail climbs to the brink of 317ft **Vernal Fall★** (1.5mi). Ambitious hikers may proceed to the top of 594ft Nevada Fall (3mi). A farther trail continues to the summit of **Half Dome★★★** (8.2mi) a massive rock that rises 4,800 vertical feet above the northeast end of the valley. The final assault of the summit (hiking permit required) mounts a 45-degree granite slab with the aid of an exposed cable ladder.

Tunnel View★★★ — From this stupendous viewpoint at the east end of the Wawona Tunnel, visitors gaze eastward into Yosemite Valley. Its portals on the south by **Cathedral Rocks** and on the north by the massive 3,593ft face of **El Capitan★★**,

Sunken garden, Filoli

Saxon Holt/Filoli

unbroken mountain range in the continental US.

It contains the highest US summit outside of Alaska, one of the deepest canyons and highest waterfalls as well as the largest national parks.

Yosemite National Park ★★★

This sprawling national park encompasses 1,770sq mi of pristine forests, groves of giants sequoias, alpine lakes, abundant

the world's largest unbroken cliff. Graceful **Bridalveil Fall** hangs in the foreground. The distinctive, sheer face of Half Dome peers round the shoulder of Glacier Point from the eastern end of the valley.

Glacier Point★★★ — *30mi south and east from Yosemite village; 0.2mi walk from parking area.* One of the nation's most spectacular viewpoints, this rocky peak hovers 3,000ft above the valley floor. From here, Vernal and Nevada Falls and Little Yosemite Valley are visible to the east behind looming Half Dome, while Yosemite Falls pours down a cliff face to the northwest.

Mariposa Grove of Big Trees★★ — *34mi south of Yosemite Village. Tours by foot or tram (May-Oct, conditions permitting).* The largest of the park's three groves of giant sequoias spreads over 250 acres of a steep hillside. Most massive of nearly 400 mature sequoias is the **Grizzly Giant,** a 2,700-year-old specimen with a base circumference of 96ft and a pronounced lean of 17 degrees. The adjacent **California Tunnel Tree** was bored in 1895 to allow coaches to pass through it, a fashionable novelty of Victorian tourism.

Tioga Road★★ — *62mi one-way north and east from Yosemite Village to Tioga Pass. Last 45mi (past Crane Flat) closed Nov-late May.* Rte 120 snakes 14mi through thick evergreen forests before opening to broad views of the high country. **Olmstead Point★** provides striking vistas down Tenaya Canyon to Half Dome and Clouds Rest (9,926ft). Passing subalpine **Tenaya Lake,** the largest natural body of water in the park, the road enters **Tuolumne Meadows★★,** an alpine grassland at 8,600ft elevation, braided by the Tuolumne River. Tuolumne offers rustic lodging and dining, a visitor center, and access to miles of backcountry trails. A marvelous short trail climbs to the glacier-polished summit of 9,450ft **Lembert Dome★** (3mi roundtrip). Beyond 9,945ft **Tioga Pass★,** the highest roadway pass in the state, Rte. 120 escends 13 mi to the junction of US-395 near Mono Lake.

EXCURSIONS

wildlife and awe-inspiring peaks. Ice Age glaciers grinding down the Merced River canyon scooped out Yosemite's distinctive U-shaped trough, 7mi long and more than 4,000ft deep, sculpting monumental rocks and polishing cliffs where steams now plummet as waterfalls. The native Ahwahneechee people were forced to surrender Yosemite to Europeans and American pioneers in 1851; just 13 years later, the federal government set aside Yosemite Valley and the Wawona Grove as a natural preserve. The effusive writings of naturalist John Muir prompted Congress in 1890 to preserve the surrounding wilderness as Yosemite National Park.

Today, millions of visitors come each year to hike, backpack, bicycle, fish, ride horseback, camp, ski or simply drink in the magnificent scenery. Though it constitutes less than 6 percent of the park's land area, Yosemite Valley remains the principal attraction. Visitors may tour the east end of the valley aboard a free shuttle bus.

Lake Tahoe★★

Encircled by a ring of lofty ridges and peaks, this deep blue lake straddling the California-Nevada border at 6,225ft elevation is the most popular resort area in the Sierra. The lake basin was once the summering ground of the Washoe people. It was rapidly claimed and developed after the discovery of the Comstock Lode, when its broad surface was used by steamboats that transported timber to shore up the mines. **South Lake Tahoe,**

a small city of motels, shops and restaurants, serves vacationers who flock for summer recreation, winter skiing, and casino entertainment. Highways encircle the lake, linking numerous ski resorts and smaller rustic settlements geared for summer visits. Trailheads offer access to excellent hiking, including the 150mi **Tahoe Rim Trail,** which encircles the lake near the ridgeline.

By riding the spectacular cable car at **Squaw Valley** (530-583-6985), visitors can enjoy splendid views from the 8,200ft-elevation sundeck at **High Camp★**. Skiing and snowboarding provide winter sport at Squaw Valley, site of the 1960 Winter Olympics. Another splendid view of Lake Tahoe, this one from the south, rewards riders who ascend 10,167ft Monument Peak on the **Heavenly Gondola★★** (530-586-7000).

Lake Tahoe Basin Visitors Center
870 Emerald Bay Rd. (Rte. 89),
⊘ *2.5mi northwest of South Lake Tahoe.* 530-265-4531. *www.r5.fs.fed.us/tahoe.*
This US Forest Service center provides a comprehensive overview of Tahoe's human and natural history. The Rainbow Trail (.5mi) leads from the visitor center to the Stream Profile Center, where visitors may observe fish in a mountain creek from an underwater window.

In mid-autumn, thousands of flaming red kokanee salmon spawn upstream from Lake Tahoe. The trail to **Tallac Historic Site★** leads to the remains of a fashionable 19C resort hotel and casino built by mining speculator

Emerald Bay, Lake Tahoe

Lucky Baldwin. Other private estates farther east from Baldwin's are now likewise owned by the Forest Service, which maintains the Pope-Tevis Estate (1899) and Valhalla mansion (1924) and opens the Baldwin-McGonagle House (1921) in summer as a museum.

Emerald Bay State Park★★
Emerald Bay Rd. ⟳ *(Rte.89), 8mi northwest of South Lake Tahoe.* *530-541-3030. www.parks.ca.gov.* Embracing a glacier-carved fjord acclaimed as the loveliest corner of the lake, this park provides majestic alpine views, beautiful hiking trails and guided tours of a strikingly eccentric mansion, **Vikingsholm★★** (1929), designed to resemble a 9C Nordic castle. The 5.3mi lakeshore Rubicon Trail leads across the northern edge of Emerald Bay to Lester Beach in **D.L. Bliss State Park★**.

Donner Memorial State Park★
⟳ *Off I-80 at Rte.89, 2.3 mi west of Truckee.* *530-582-7892. www.parks.ca.gov.* Commemorating the Donner Party disaster of 1846–47, the centerpiece of this ironically peaceful park on the shore of Donner Lake is a bronze statue of a family in the desperate straits of starvation.

When caught by early snows while attempting to cross the 7,239ft Donner Pass, the party of 87 emigrants, stranded without adequate provisions, erected makeshift cabins and settled in to await rescue as a smaller party set out for help. Before their rescuers returned in mid-February, the survivors were forced to cannibalize their dead; only 47 survived the ordeal. Their story is related in exhibits and film at the park's **Emigrant Trail Museum★★**.

FOR FUN

Face it, there are some things that you must do while you're in San Francisco, no matter how touristy they are. So, come on and join the crowds riding the cable cars and photographing the crookedest street. At day's end, stop for a drink in one of the city's classic watering holes and take advantage of some eye-popping views. When all is said and done, you'll be glad you did.

Ride the Cable Cars ★★★

Riding a cable car is a classic San Francisco experience, and something the whole family will enjoy. The city's celebrated open-air cable-car system provides access to many tourist attractions, notably Chinatown, Union Square and Fisherman's Wharf.

Today 40 cars climb San Francisco's hilly streets along three lines—Powell-Mason, Powell-Hyde and California Street—using the mechanism developed in 1873 by Andrew Hallidie (*see Museums; see Practical Information for details about how to ride*).

Cable Cars

Seth Affoumado/SFCVB

Drive Down the "World's Crookedest Street" ★★★

The one-lane brick-paved 1000 block of **Lombard Street** ★★★ in the Russian Hill neighborhood takes eight—count 'em—unbelievably tight hairpin turns as it makes its way down from Hyde to Leavenworth Street (*see Landmarks*). Drive it for yourself, or walk up the stairs that flank switchbacks filled with flower beds.

Take in the Best Views

Postcard Row ★★★
710-720 Steiner St. between Hayes & Grove Sts.
One of the most photographed tableaux in the city, these seven pastel-painted Victorians—together nicknamed "Postcard Row"—appear pressed against a backdrop of twinkling skyscrapers. It's a trick of the landscape, of course; the slow uphill climb from the bay to Golden Gate Park makes the Financial District appear closer than it really is, almost as if the whole scene were being viewed through a zoom lens. **Alamo Square ★**, banked up from the street on the west side of Steiner, allows photographers ample time to focus.

Twin Peaks ★★★
From Haight St., drive south on Clayton St., cross Carmel St. and continue up Twin Peaks Blvd. to Christmas Tree Point parking area on the left; or take the No. 37 bus.
At 908ft (north peak) and 922ft (south peak), these twin summits offer **panoramic views ★★★** of the city and beyond. Brace yourself for large crowds, especially on summer weekends, and dress warmly; strong, cold winds are common year-round.

Postcard Row, Alamo Square

Christine Krieg/SFCVB

Catch a Giants Game at AT&T Park ★★

3rd & King Sts., at the Embarcadero. 415-972-2000. www.sfgiants.com.
Baseball fans won't want to miss the opportunity to see the 2010 World Series champions play ball in this $319 million, 40,800-seat stadium (2000), which was designed to shield players and spectators from wind and fog, while still offering beautiful views of the bay. If you can't make a game, ballpark tours are held daily at 10:30am and 12:30pm *($12.50 Adults, $10.50 Seniors, $7.50 Kids 12 and under, free for kids 2 and under)*. During the 90-minute tour you'll visit the dugouts, press box, visitors' clubhouse, the field warning track, and indoor batting cages. At the Coca-Cola Fan Lot (on the Promenade level above the left-field bleachers), pint-size fans can slide into home plate through pop-bottle slides and run the bases at Little Giants Field, a 50-by-50ft replica of AT&T Park.

Sunsets and Sea Lions at Cliff House ★

1090 Point Lobos Ave., off 39th Ave. 415-386-3330. www.cliffhouse.com.

Ignore the busloads of tourists. **Cliff House★**, which hugs a high bluff above the Pacific Ocean in Sutro Heights, has long been a favorite spot to catch ocean breezes and **stunning views ★★** up the rocky coast.
Bring binoculars to spy on the raucous sea lions that roost offshore on Seal Rocks and stay to watch the sunset.

Cocktails With A View

Drink in some of the city's best **views★★★** with your cocktail in one of Nob Hills' premier historic hotels. At the InterContinental Mark Hopkins Hotel *(999 California St.; 415-616-6916; www.intercontinentalmarkhopkins.com/top_of_the_mark)*, the **Top of the Mark** lounge has crowned the 19th floor since 1939. Go for drinks and light dining *(see Nightlife)*, afternoon tea (Mon–Sat) or the Sunday champagne brunch.

FOR FUN

MUSTS FOR OUTDOOR FUN

Surrounded by water and bordered to the north by the Marin Headlands (on the other side of the Golden Gate Bridge), San Francisco offers some great opportunities for recreation. Grab a bike or a pair of sneakers and exercise your heart out—just walking up and down the city's hilly streets is a workout in itself! If it's relaxation you crave, hop on a cruise boat or just chill out at the beach.

Marin Headlands

©mtilghma/iStockphoto.com

Cruise the Bay★★

Getting out on the blue waters of San Francisco Bay makes a wonderful family excursion on a warm, sunny day and gives you a whole new perspective of the city skyline and the Golden Gate Bridge. Whether you just cruise the bay, sail under the bridge, or go to Alcatraz (see Landmarks) or Sausalito (see Excursions), you can't beat the **views★★★** from the water.

Walk the Coastal Trail★★

Trail starts at far end of the Merrie Way parking lot next to Cliff House (west end of Point Lobos Ave.). 415-561-4700. www.nps.gov/goga.

Part of the Golden Gate National Recreation Area, this 3.5mi loop trail makes for an invigorating walk along San Francisco's northwesternmost headland. On a clear day, the wild, heavily wooded shoreline here provides **spectacular views★★★** of the ocean, the Golden Gate Bridge and the Marin Headlands. Eucalyptus trees scent the hills rising to the south, while Monterey pines and firs hold the crumbling cliffs in place with their gnarled roots. The winding main trail leads to a

Tips for Cruising

Two major cruise lines, the **Blue and Gold Fleet** and the **Red and White Fleet**, both depart from piers at Fisherman's Wharf (see Landmarks). Tours are narrated and last about an hour. In season, it's best to book in advance. Call or check the fleets' Web sites for schedules.

♦ **Blue and Gold Fleet** departs from Pier 39. 415-705-8200. www.blueandgold fleet.com. $24 Adult, $20 Senior, $20 Junior (12-18), $16 Child (5-11). Save $2 when purchasing tickets online or receive the Family Discount price (2 Adults and up to 4 Children) for $70. Available only at Pier 39 box office.

♦ **Red and White Fleet** leaves from Pier 43. 415-673-2900. www.redandwhite fleet.com. $24 Adult (18+), $16 Youth (5-17). $69 Family Price (2 Adults and 4 Youth)

MUST DO

viewing platform overlooking the posh Sea Cliff neighborhood. The return route takes you through Lincoln Park Golf Course and past the California Palace of the Legion of Honor (see Museums) before ending at the Fort Miley parking lot.

Angel Island State Park★★

Access to the island is by private boat or public ferry from San Francisco. 415-435-5390. www.parks.ca.gov.

This hilly, forested island in San Francisco Bay served as a missile-launching base for the US military and as an immigration facility before it became part of the California state park system in 1963. Today you can explore the island by foot, by bike or by one-hour tram tour (call the Cove Café for current day's schedule; 415-435-3392; Angel Island TramTours; www.angelisland.com). More adventurous souls can try the 2 ½-hour sea kayak tour (Sea Trek Ocean Kayaking; 415-488-1000; www.seatrek kayak.com). Sandy unguarded beaches at **Quarry Point** and **Ayala Cove** (site of the park visitor center) are both good for picnicking and sunbathing (caution: swim at your own risk—currents are strong). From Ayala Cove you can access the 5mi Perimeter Road that loops around the island, and the rugged trail that climbs to the 781ft summit of Mount Livermore, where you'll have a **panoramic view ★★★** of the Bay area.

Battery Ledyard, Angel Island

Angel Island Company

Angel Island Ferry

The Angel Island Ferry is operated year-round by the Blue and Gold Fleet. The hop from Pier 41 on Fisherman's Wharf to Angel Island takes only 20 minutes (round-trip fare $16 adults, $9 children age 6–11); schedules: 415-705-5555 or www.blueandgoldfleet.com; no weekday service to the island in winter).

🛶 Spend an Afternoon at Ocean Beach★

Although the chilling waters of the Pacific might not tempt you, the best option for beaching it in the city is the broad expanse of sand at **Ocean Beach★**, where San Francisco meets the sea. Part of the Golden Gate National Recreational Area, Ocean Beach extends from Cliff House (end of Point Lobos Ave., off 39th Ave.) 4mi south to Fort Funston. It's a great place to walk and jog—or sunbathe and picnic when it's not too windy—but swimming's not recommended in the rough surf (there are no lifeguards). Surfers are among the few who brave the dangerous riptides here. At sunset, park in lots along the Great Highway and watch the sun sink slowly in the west.

FOR KIDS

You'd expect a city with such a free-wheeling spirit to love to play around. And San Francisco does just that: from the Pier 39 arcades to the zoo, kids of all ages—and young-at-heart adults—will find an ABCs full of fun in the City by the Bay. Here are a few of our favorites:

Golden Gate Park★★★ for Kids

Bounded by Fulton St., Lincoln Way, Stanyan St. & Great Hwy. 415-831-2700. www.parks.sfgov.org.

The park's 1,017 acres offer plenty of space for recreation, from ball fields to formal gardens. Several of its attractions will appeal particularly to children.

California Academy of Sciences

55 Concourse Dr. Golden Gate Park. Open year-round Mon–Sat 9:30am–5pm, Sun 11am–5pm. Closed Thanksgiving Day, Dec 25. Adult $29.95, ages 12–17 $24.95, ages 4-11 $19.95. 415-379-8000. www.calacademy.org.

The Steinhart Aquarium houses some 38,000 live animals, representing nearly 1,000 species, from African penguins to sharks, stingrays, and colorful reef fish in the large Philippine Coral Reef exhibit. Meanwhile, the Academy's four-story rainforest exhibit is home to free-flying birds and butterflies, a Borneo bat cave, an Amazonian flooded forest, and exotic reptiles and amphibians.

Children's Playground

East side of the park at Martin Luther King, Jr. Dr. & Bowling Green Dr.

Kids love to monkey around on the slides, swings and climbing structures here. Be sure to save time for a ride on the magnificently restored 1912 **carrousel**★. Creative types can attend art classes in the 1888 Sharon Building, now the Sharon Arts Studio *(for schedules, call 415-753-7004; www.sharon artstudio.org).*

Exploratorium★★

3601 Lyon St., at the Palace of Fine Arts (see Landmarks). 415-561-0399. www.exploratorium.edu. Open year-round Tue–Sun 10am–5pm. Closed Mon, Thanksgiving Day & Dec 25. Adults $15, ages 13-17 $12, ages 4-12 $10, free first Wed of every month.

Science comes to life in hundreds of interactive stations inside the Palace of Fine Arts. By pushing buttons, rotating wheels, peering through prisms, and performing a host of other actions, you set experiments in motion and observe the results. Over 400 exhibits on view cover a range of subject areas, including human perception (such as vision, hearing, learning

Exploratorium

©Amy Snyder/Exploratorium

Golden Gate Park Carousel

Carousels

Forget about thrill rides—who doesn't love an old-fashioned carousel? The 1912 Herschell-Spillman Company **Carousel★** in **Golden Gate Park** was featured in the 1939 World's Fair on Treasure Island. It boasts a menagerie of 62 brightly painted wooden animals. *Open daily, Memorial Day–Labor Day and open Fri–Sun for the rest of the year. Rides run from 10am–4:30 pm. $2 Adults $1 Kids (6–12) Free (under 5).* On the **Rooftop at Yerba Buena Gardens** you'll find a hand-carved carousel that was made in 1906. Its stable of 65 fanciful creatures is enclosed in a glass pavilion *(Fourth & Howard Sts.; open 11am–6pm daily; $3 for 2 rides).* The city's newest carousel, made in Italy, debuted at the north end of **Pier 39** in 2002 *(open Sun–Thu 10am–8pm, Fri & Sat 10am–9pm; $3).*

and cognition), the life sciences, and physical phenomena (such as light, motion, electricity, waves and resonance, and weather).

If you're not claustrophobic, try crawling through the multilevel Tactile Dome; inside it's pitch-black and soundproof, so you have to feel your way through.

Rooftop at Yerba Buena Gardens★★

Bounded by Mission, Folsom, Third & Fourth Sts. Entrances on Mission, Howard & Third Sts. 415-820-3550. www.yerbabuenagardens.com. Open year-round daily 6am–10pm.

At this two-block square urban park devoted to the younger set, kids can splash in a stream, romp in a 100,000sq ft children's garden,

get lost in a hedge labyrinth, ice-skate year-round, go bowling, and ride a 1906 carousel (see above)—and that's just for starters.

Zeum★

415-820-3320. www.zeum.org. Open mid-Jun–Aug Tue–Sun 11am–5pm. Rest of the year Wed - Fri, 1pm-5pm Sat - Sun, 11am-5pm. $10 Adults, $8 Youth (3-18), $8 Students/Seniors.

If you can dream it, you can do it at Zeum's 34,000sq ft production facility. Budding artists can draw, sculpt and paint; young animators can create flip-book or claymation cartoons; and little ones who crave the limelight can produce and star in their own videos.

FOR KIDS

Ghirardelli Square

Ghirardelli Square

Ghirardelli Chocolate Manufactory and Soda Fountain

Ghirardelli Square, 900 North Point St., 415-474-3938. www.ghirardelli.com. Open year-round daily 9am-11pm (Fri & Sat until midnight). Ice Cream Fountain opens at 10am daily.

It's always time for a hot fudge sundae—and what better place to get one than at the soda fountain of San Francisco's venerable chocolate maker? Located in the city since 1895, Ghirardelli satisfies sweet tooths with confections

made with the company's yummy chocolate. Slurp a shake, lick a cone, sip a hot chocolate, but don't attempt the Earthquake— a gargantuan sundae with eight scoops, eight toppings, bananas, nuts and cherries—without reinforcements. Chocolate to go is available at the on-site store.

San Francisco Fire Engine Tours

Tours depart from the Cannery at Fisherman's Wharf (Beach St. at the foot of Columbus St.) year-round Wed–Mon at 1pm. 415-333-7077. www.fireenginetours.com. Reservations required. $50 adults, $40 teens (ages 13–17), $30 children.

A good time is guaranteed for all on this unique excursion. Put on your fireman's gear, board a 1955 Big Red Shiny Mack Fire Engine and join the crew in song! During the 75-minute sightseeing tour, you'll ride across the Golden Gate Bridge and stop at Fort Baker for a great photo op of the bright orange span.

More Fun on the Pier

But wait, there's more! For little ones there's the **carousel**; olders will get a kick out of the virtual-reality **Turbo Ride 4D** *(415-392-8872)*. Nearby, at Pier 45, play vintage penny arcade games at **Musee Mechanique** *(415-346-2000, www.museemechanique.com, Mon–Fri 10am–7pm, Sat–Sun 10am–8pm)*.

MUST DO

🦀 Pier 39★

Beach St. at the Embarcadero. 415-981-7437. www.pier39.com. Attractions & shops open year-round daily 10am–8pm (hours vary seasonally).

Pier 39 packs oodles of entertainment for the whole family into its festival marketplace. Be sure to meet the resident "sea-lebrities"—the **noisy sea lions★** that hang out near K Dock (free educational talks on weekends, 11am–5pm).

Aquarium of the Bay★

On the east side of the pier entrance. 888-732-3483. www.aquariumofthebay.com. Summer: 9am–8pm, Fall/Spring: Mon–Thur 10am–7pm Fri–Sun 10am–8pm. Winter: Mon–Thur 10am–6pm Fri–Sun 10am–7pm. $16.95 Adults, $8 Children/Seniors.

Eels, octopi, skates, rays, jelly fish, sharks, sea stars, and other denizens of the waters in and around San Francisco Bay will swim around you as you walk through the clear tunnels on the lower level of the three-story aquarium. Some 20,000 aquatic animals from nearly 200 different species are showcased here; at touch tables you'll have a chance to meet some of them face-to-face.

San Francisco Zoo★

Sloat Blvd. at 47th Ave. (vehicle entrance off the Great Hwy.). 415-753-7080. www.sfzoo.org. Open daily 10am–5pm (Nov 7–Mar 11 until 4pm). $15 Adult (5–64) $9 Children (4–14) Free (3 and under) $12 Seniors.

Set on 125 acres south of Golden Gate Park, the zoo focuses on naturalistic habitats for some 250 species. Highlights include the Lipman Family Lemur Forest (the country's largest outdoor lemur habitat), Penguin Island, a pair of grizzly bears, the African Savanna exhibit (complete with giraffe, zebra, kudu and oryx) and the six-acre Children's Zoo *(open daily 10am–4pm)*.

African Savanna Exhibit, San Francisco Zoo

San Francisco Zoo

FOR KIDS

PERFORMING ARTS

Famed for its cultural diversity, San Francisco has always been a hotbed for performance. From a cappella to zydeco, you're sure to find something to suit your taste and pocketbook. Check local papers or sfarts.org for this week's events and critics' picks.

MUSIC AND DANCE

San Francisco Ballet

War Memorial Opera House, 301 Van Ness Ave. (at Grove St). 415-865-2000. www.sfballet.org. Season: Feb–May.

The innovative ballet—the first professional company in the US—still ranks among the country's best, alongside New York City Ballet and American Ballet Theater. It is particularly acclaimed for its interpretations of works by George Balanchine.

San Francisco Opera

War Memorial Opera House, 301 Van Ness Ave. (at Grove St). 415-864-3330. http://sfopera.com. Season: Jun–July & Sept–Dec.

Of all the musical arts, opera is the one that has most enduringly won a place in San Francisco's heart. Decades before the city got a reputation for being "artsy," gold miners were getting an earful of Bellini. Today the company, widely recognized as the best on the West Coast, performs in the sumptuous War Memorial Opera House *(see Neighborhoods/Civic Center).*

San Francisco Symphony

Louise M. Davies Symphony Hall, 201 Van Ness Ave. 415-864-6000. www.sfsymphony.org. Season: Sept–July.

The appointment of the dashing Michael Tilson Thomas as symphony director was hailed as the cultural event of 1995. An ardent champion of American composers, this Leonard Bernstein protégé has brought Aaron Copland, John Adams, Samuel Barber and, yes, Leonard Bernstein into the rotation, along with so-called "difficult" composers Gustav Mahler, Hector Berlioz and Rimsky-Korsakov.

THEATER AND INTERDISCIPLINARY ARTS

Curran Theatre★

445 Geary Blvd. 415-551-2000. www.shnsf.com/theatres/curran.

Producers Carole Shorenstein Hays and Scott E. Nederlander

Davies Symphony Hall

Courtesy San Francisco Symphony

MUST DO

present their "Best of Broadway" series at the Curran, the Golden Gate Theater (1 Taylor St.), and the Orpheum Theatre (1192 Market St.). The fare consists of long-running musicals such as Mamma Mia!, Hairspray and The Lion King.

Geary Theater★

415 Geary St. 415-749-2228. http://act-sf.org.

This sumptuous 1909 landmark is home to the Actors Conservatory Theater (ACT), widely regarded as the best company in the city, with stellar performances and inventive stage sets. In a typical seven-play season, you're likely to see Charles Dickens' A Christmas Carol; works by well-known contemporary writers, such as William Saroyan; and world premieres of new works.

Zeum★

221 4th St., in Yerba Buena Gardens. 415-820-3320. www.zeum.org.

The 210-seat theater is used by ACT (see Geary Theater, above) for developing new works and staging small company productions, many with a multicultural focus.

Berkeley Repertory Theater

2025 Addison St., Berkeley. 510-647-2949. www.berkeleyrep.org Season: Sept–July.

Established in 1968, the Tony Award-winning theater puts on six to seven shows a season, a mix of classics and new plays.

Magic Theatre

Fort Mason, Building D. 415-441-8822. www.magictheatre.org.

Founded in a Berkeley bar in 1967 by director John Lion and a group of actors, the Magic is now situated in San Francisco's Marina District. It has a long history of introducing new works, including Sam Shepard's True West, Fool for Love, and Pulitzer Prize-winning Buried Child, as well as the first plays of Nilo Cruz, who won the 2003 Pulitzer.

San Francisco Performances

Box office: 415-392-2545. www.performances.org. Season: Sept–May.

For 24 years this group has been bringing the world's best singers, musicians, dancers and writers to the city for short-term engagements. Many of the season's 200 performances are staged at the Civic Center's Herbst Theatre.

Yerba Buena Center for the Arts Theater

701 Mission St. (at 3rd St). 415-978-2787. ybca.org.

Multiculturalism reigns at this new, 750-seat theater. Recent performances have included Chinese opera, African dance and new plays.

NIGHTLIFE

Some folks might grumble about the relatively early last call (2am) at San Francisco's bars, but you don't hear many complaints about the quality and character of its establishments. Nearly every neighborhood has its local hangout from dive bars to chic wine bars and danceclubs.

Bars and Pubs

Bubble Lounge
714 Montgomery St., Financial District. 415-434-4204. www.bubblelounge.com.
Flutes of cold bubbly can be sipped on plush couches and overstuffed chairs, or just enjoy the dance floor.

Café du Nord
2170 Market St., Castro District. 415-861-5016. www.cafedunord.com.
Mahogany and velvet dominate the decor at this swank former speakeasy.

Dalva
3121 16th St., Mission District. 415-252-7740.
Reputed to have the best jukebox in town, this dim railroad flat of a

bar celebrates happy hour each day from 4pm to 7pm with $2 pints, well mixed drinks, and sangria.

Orbit Room
1900 Market St., Castro District. 415-252-9525.
Retro rules at this sleek corner bar, where the service is friendly, the music is mellow (oldies, of course), and the cocktails are works of art. Don't be surprised to see a fleet of Vespas parked outside.

Specs'
12 William Saroyan Pl. 415-421-4112.
Formally called Specs' Twelve Adler Museum Cafe, Richard "Specs" Simmons' maritime-themed hole-in-the-wall has local color (and locals) a-plenty.

Tonga Room
Fairmont Hotel, California & Powell Sts., Nob Hill. 415-772-5278. www.tongaroom.com.
Thatched umbrellas hover over rustic tables and bedeck nearly all the drinks at this kitschy Polynesian bar, a Nob Hill institution with exploding volcanoes and lagoon.

Alembic
1725 Haight St. Haight-Asbury. 415-666-0822. www.alembicbar.com.
The mixologists at this cozy Upper Haight haunt are experts at their art, mixing up sazeracs, pisco sours and Blood and Sands (scotch

---

Cinephiles, Unite!

Clubs aren't your idea of fun? You're not alone. Thousands of the hippest hipsters in San Francisco flock to the movies, even on weekend nights. A good place to get your cine-fix is the 1,500-seat **Castro Theatre★** (429 Castro St.; 415-621-6120; www.thecastrotheatre.com). Decked out in gold leaf and velvet swag, this is a movie palace nonpareil. Foreign films, classics and rare oldies all make it to the mammoth screen here, as do new works from several annual film festivals.

whiskey, cherry brandy, sweet vermouth and orange juice).

Bourbon & Branch
501 Jones St., at O'Farrell, Downtown. 415-931-7292. www.bourbonandbranch.com.
This sultry speakeasy in the Tenderloin has no sign (look for the door below the Anti-Saloon League sign) and you have to ring a buzzer to get in. Make reservations for the main room, or say the password "Books" to gain admittance into the Library bar.

Cantina
580 Sutter St., Downtown. 415-398-0195. www.cantinasf.com.
Weekend nights find a full house at this Latin-inspired lounge near Union Square, where caipirinhas, sangrias and mojitos flow.

El Rio
3158 Mission St., Mission. 415-282-3325. www.elriosf.com.
A stellar back patio draws diverse throngs to weekend salsa and burlesque shows at this friendly lower Mission bar. Nights brings DJs and live music.

La Trappe
800 Greenwich St., North Beach. 415-440-8727. www.latrappe cafe.com.
Pass through the quiet restaurant and descend the spiral staircase to enter this Belgian beer den, which buzzes on weekend nights.

Rickhouse
246 Kearny St., Financial District. 415-398-2827. www.rickhouse bar.com.
A prime place for post-work mingling, this downtown bar is

packed with professionals on weeknights. The small loft often has more breathing room.

Toronado
547 Haight St., Lower Haight. 415-863-2276. www.toronado.com.
Beloved by locals, this Lower Haight pub has great selection of brews. Bonus: they sell sausages from Rosamunde's next door.

Dance Clubs

Elbo Room
647 Valencia St., Mission District. 415-552-7788. www.elbo.com.
Reggae, hip-hop, jazz, and Brazilian bands set the crowd dancing on the second floor of this popular Mission hangout. The cover is cheap (under $10), and happy "hour" ($2 pints) is 5pm-9pm daily.

Mezzanine
444 Jessie St., SoMa. 415-820-9669.
No "hipper than thou" attitudes at this vast industrial space, where up to 900 souls have been known to crowd the dance floor at a time. The crowd is gay and straight; the DJs among the best.

111 Minna
111 Minna St., SoMa. 415-974-1719 www.111minnagallery.com. $5 cover.
Qool, the long-running Wednesday-night happy hour at this funky art gallery/night club goes until 11pm and features up to six DJs spinning everything from drum-and-bass to progressive rock.

Ruby Skye
420 Mason St. (between Geary & Post Sts.), Union Square. 415-693-0777. www.rubyskye.com.

NIGHTLIFE

Four different rooms, a bi-level dance floor and throbbing hip hop, house and techno music from live bands and DJs make this Union Square area spot popular.

Ten15 Folsom
1015 Folsom St. (between 6th & 7th Sts.), SoMa. 415-431-1200. www.1015.com.
Every big-name DJ in the world has spun here, at what some people believe is the most influential club on the West Coast. Buy tickets in advance for popular shows.

Blues, Jazz, Rock and World Music

Bimbo's 365 Club
1025 Columbus Ave., North Beach. 415-474-0365. www.bimbos365club.com.
They've been packing 'em in at this North Beach institution since 1951. The roster no longer includes jugglers, but you can still soak in the atmosphere, elegant decor and live music, from rockabilly to torch songs.

Biscuits & Blues
401 Mason St., Union Square. 415-292-2853. www.biscuitsand bluessf.com.
Tasty Southern food and down-to-earth prices add to the appeal of this cool club, which gets some of the best blues acts around. Live music nightly.

Boom Boom Room
1601 Fillmore St. 415-673-8000. www.boomboomblues.com.
Its intimate size and loyal following make John Lee Hooker's club near Japantown a draw for musicians and fans alike.

The Fillmore
1805 Geary Blvd. 415-346-6000. www.thefillmore.com.
Impresario Bill Graham turned this 1920s dancehall near Japantown into a 1960s landmark by booking acts like Janis Joplin, Jimi Hendrix, and Jefferson Airplane. Today it's a haven for alternative rock.

The Independent
628 Divisadero St. 415-771-1421. www.theindependentsf.com.
This spot seems to top everyone's list for great new bands, indie favorites and a happening crowd.

Great American Music Hall
859 O'Farrell St., Tenderloin. 415-885-0750. www.musichallsf.com.
Soaring marble columns, an oak dance floor and an ornate wraparound balcony make this gorgeous 1907 nightclub one of the best places in town to see a show. The fare includes indie rock, and there's a full-service kitchen.

Lou's Pier 47
300 Jefferson St., Fisherman's Wharf. 415-771-5687. www.louspier47.com.
For those who think that the best places are tucked behind unmarked doors in obscure neighborhoods, take a look at Lou's. Right in the thick of Pier 39 mania, Lou's serves Cajun food downstairs, blues and jazz upstairs.

Slim's
333 11th St., SoMa. 415-255-0333. www.slims-sf.com.
Billed as the "home of roots music," this San Francisco institution, partially owned by rocker Boz Scaggs, has recently hosted the Psychedelic Furs, John Zorn, and

the Knitters. The space is boxy and tends to be loud, so bring ear plugs—or buy them at the bar.

Yoshi's
510 Embarcadero W. (Jack London Square), Oakland. 510-238-9200. 2nd address: 1330 Fillmore Street, 415-655-5600. www.yoshis.com.
Located in Oakland's Jack London Square area, the top venue for jazz in the Bay Area opened a San Francisco outpost in 2007. The cabaret-style theaters, open nightly, presents world-class acts. Advance tickets recommended.

Cabaret and Piano Bars

Harry Denton's Starlight Room
Sir Francis Drake Hotel, 450 Powell St., Union Square. 415-395-8595. www.harrydenton.com.
Harry, the expansive proprietor, invites you to come for the views and stay for the entertainment at his ritzy rooftop nightclub. The four-piece Starlight Orchestra sets the crowd to dancing every Thursday to Saturday night (reservations recommended).

Top of the Mark
Intercontinental Mark Hopkins Hotel, One Nob Hill. 415-616-6916. www.topofthemark.com.
Perhaps the most famous bar in San Francisco offers 360-degree **views★★★**, perfectly poured martinis and a festive atmosphere. On Friday and Saturday nights, dance cheek to cheek to the music of the Black Market Jazz Orchestra. "Smart casual" dress after 8:30pm.

Comedy Clubs

Cobb's Comedy Club
915 Columbus Ave., North Beach. 415-928-4320. www.cobbscomedy club.com. Closed Mon & Tue.
To take the stage at Cobb's you must have performed on *The Tonight Show with Jay Leno, Late Night with Conan O'Brien, HBO/ Showtime Comedy Showcase*, or in a major feature film. Wednesday's comedy showcase is a steal at $7.

Punch Line
444 Battery St., 2nd floor, Financial District. 415-397-7573. www.punchlinecomedyclub.com.
The Punch Line draws the funniest of the funny: Robin Williams, Ellen Degeneres, Rosie O'Donnell, Drew Carey, Chris Rock and Dana Carvey have all crossed the stage here. Today, the club hosts the likes of Dave Chappelle and Jay Mohr.

Beach Blanket Babylon
Club Fugazi, 678 Beach Blanket Babylon St. (formerly Green St.), North Beach. 415-421-4222. www.beachblanketbabylon.com.
Where else can you find Paris Hilton and Oprah Winfrey, Martha Stewart and Arnold Schwarzenegger, J.Lo and Eminem—and some of the most ludicrous hats ever created—together on the same stage? This outrageous spoof of current events and pop culture has played before packed houses eight times weekly since 1974, when it was hatched by impresario Steve Silver. It is acclaimed as the longest-running musical review in history.

NIGHTLIFE

SHOPPING

For all its anti-materialist pretensions, San Francisco is a terrific shopping city, catering to every taste and budget. You can get just about anything here if you know where to look, and looking is half the fun of it. In a city without a bad angle, shopkeepers know the virtue of stylish presentation.

The Cannery★★

2801 Leavenworth St. 415-771-3112. www.thecannery.com.

Built in 1907, this handsome brick building housed the most productive peach-canning operation in the world from 1916 to 1937. It was remodeled in 1968 as an airy, three-level retail and entertainment complex with a flower-filled sunken courtyard.

Ferry Building Marketplace★★

Embarcadero at Market St. www.ferrybuildingmarketplace.com.

The soaring central arcade of the renovated **1898 Ferry Building★★** (see Landmarks) was recently transformed into a stunning showcase for the region's finest food. Think artisan cheeses from Cow Girl Creamery, 50 flavors of hand-made gelato from Ciao Bella,

25 varieties of organic peaches from Frog Hollow Farm, and handmade bonbons from Recchiuti Confections. San Francisco City Guides give free 45-minute tours of the Ferry Building (samples included!) on Tuesdays, Thursdays, and Saturdays *(415-557-4266; www.sfcityguides.org)*. Across the street, **carrousel★** *(415-772-0700; www.embarcadero center.com)* holds more than 125 stores in a four-structure complex linked by pedestrian bridges.

Ghirardelli Square★★

900 North Point St. between Polk & Larkin Sts. 415-474-3938. www.ghirardellisq.com.

Four decades after it spearheaded the revitalization of the waterfront, this 1864 chocolate factory still attracts flocks of visitors. Exposed brick walls and hardwood floors have been preserved throughout the interior, now packed with boutiques. Don't leave without sampling some goodies

Outdoor market, Ferry Building

Peter Wrenn/MICHELIN

Maiden Lane

Off Stockton St., between Geary & Post Sts. Once lined by brothels, this charming street was reincarnated after the 1906 fire as a quaint pedestrian lane. Today designer boutiques, salons and galleries fill its storefronts.

MUST DO

Ferry Plaza Farmers' Market

At the Ferry Building. 415-291-3276. www.ferryplazafarmersmarket.com. Call or check Web site for schedules. This festive outdoor market operates year-round, drawing farmers, chefs and food lovers from all over the Bay Area. The large **Saturday market★**, which takes place on the rear plaza overlooking the bay (8am–2pm), teems with tables heaped with organic produce (think white, red, and orange carrots; magenta-fleshed heirloom watermelon radishes), mouth-watering baked goods, fresh pasta and much more.

from the Ghirardelli Chocolate Manufactory and Soda Fountain *(see For Kids)*.

🛍 Union Square★★

Bounded by Sutter, Taylor, Kearny & O'Farrell Sts. www.unionsquareshop.com.

San Francisco's ritziest retail district centers on a palm- and poppy-laden plaza, where the city sponsors free concerts and events throughout the year.
The Westin St. Francis Hotel looms over its western edge (see Landmarks and Must Stay), and upscale department stores flank other sides of the square: Macy's West and Neiman Marcus on the south side, and Saks Fifth Avenue on the north. Well-heeled fashionistas flock to Union Square in search of the perfect handbag, a couture ball gown, or a diamond necklace.
Even if you can't afford to buy, it's still fun to window-shop.
A few blocks away is the **Westfield San Francisco Centre** *(865 Market St.; 415-495-5656),* an enormous complex of more than 170 shops and restaurants, the top five floors of which are occupied by the tony department store Nordstrom. **Bloomingdale's** *(415-856-5300)* anchors the Westfield's new extension, which also hosts a Burke

Union Square and Westin St. Francis Hotel

Brigitta L. House/MICHELIN

Williams spa, a movie theater, and a large basement-level food court.

A Union Square Shopping Sampler
The list of chic shops surrounding Union Square reads like a who's who of big-name designers:

- **Cartier** – *231 Post St. 415-397-3180. www.cartier.com.* French jewels for the very, very well-to-do.
- **Gucci** – *200 Stockton St. 415-392-2808. www.gucci.com.* Brown and tan with G's all over, the pimply leather of a Gucci bag is unmistakable.
- **Gump's** – *250 Post St. 415-982-1616. www.gumps.com.* The East-meets-West interior design gallery has been a San Francisco fixture for 150 years.

- **Hermès of Paris** – *125 Grant Ave. 415-391-7200. www.hermes.com.* Elegant scarves, gloves and leather goods, including saddles.
- **Wilkes Bashford** – *375 Sutter St. 415-986-4380. www.wilkes bashford.com.* This beloved local haberdashery has some of the most inventive window displays in the neighborhood. Antiques fill the basement.

Best Neighborhoods for Shopping

Chinatown★★★

Grant Ave. between Bush & Jackson Sts.

Just north of the Chinatown Gate, **Grant Avenue★★** explodes with shops selling trinkets, jewelry, artwork, electronics, bamboo and ceramics. The **China Trade Center mall** *(no. 838)* has three floors of additional stores. Stop at the **Chinatown Kite Shop** *(no. 717)* for brightly colored fish kites, box kites and windsocks.

Grant Avenue, Chinatown

Peter Wrenn/MICHELIN

Haight-Ashbury

Jack Hollingsworth/SFCVB

Haight-Ashbury★

Haight St. from Central Ave. to Stanyan St.

Clothes and music are Haight Street's major exports. **Buffalo Exchange** *(1555 Haight St.; 415-431-7733; www.buffaloexchange. com)* does a brisk trade in quality used duds—from fancy-label chic to vintage originals. **Amoeba Music** *(1855 Haight St.; 415-831-1200; amoeba.com)* has a tremendous selection of new and used CDs, DVDs and vinyl.

Pacific Heights★

Fillmore St. between Jackson & Sutter Sts.

Hang on to your wallet. You could spend a full day and a lot of cash popping in and out of the scores of the interesting shops along Fillmore Street. Here, high-end thrift stores are sprinkled among the salons, cafes, antique shops and design stores, and women's clothiers.

Mission District★

Valencia St. between 16th & 20th Sts.

Rapid dot-commification in the 1990s brought a rash of eclectic boutiques to Valencia, along with a new generation of hipsters. Styles tend toward retro and vintage, sometimes veering into kitsch.

MUST DO

🚲 Marina and Cow Hollow

Chestnut St. between Divisadero and Fillmore Sts., and Union St. between Van Ness & Steiner Sts.

The shopping scene in the northwest part of San Francisco is dominated by two main streets, Union and Chestnut. Both are host to dozens of clothing, jewelry and beauty boutiques, as well as antique stores, salons, cafés and restaurants. Among the most popular women's boutiques on **Union Street** is **Ambiance** *(1864 Union St.; 415-923-979)* offering trendy clothing, shoes and accessories.

Hayes Valley

Hayes St. from Franklin to Octavia St.

Just a stone's throw from City Hall, this once-sleepy strip now caters to chic, creatively minded locals. Trendy clothing boutiques like **Azalea** *(411 Hayes St.; 415-861-9888)* and unique home furnishing shops dominate the small Hayes Valley shopping stretch, supplemented by unique finds like the travel-oriented **Flight001** *(525 Hayes St.; 415-487-1001)* and the beauty supply shop **Nancy Boy** *(347 Hayes St.; 415-552-3802).*

Japantown

Post St. between Laguna & Fillmore Sts.

Built in 1968, Japan Center anchors the small neighborhood of Nihonmachi, or Japantown. You'll find rice cookers, woks, origami paper, kimonos, lanterns, tatami mats, and all manner of animé DVDs in this three-block shopping arcade, as well as excellent restaurants, an art-house cinema, and a soothing spa (*see Spas*).

City Lights Bookstore

©City Lights Bookstore

Bookstores

San Francisco has more bookstores per capita than any other city in the US. **City Lights★** *(261 Columbus Ave.; 415-362-8193; www.citylights. com),* founded by beat poet Lawrence Ferlinghetti in 1953, remains a North Beach landmark for its extensive poetry collection and browser-friendly atmosphere. Mergatroid, a wooden leprechaun, stands sentry outside **Green Apple** *(506 Clement St.; 415-387-2272; www.greenapplebooks.com),* a sprawling warren of creaky-floored rooms piled floor-to-ceiling with used books. Mission District fixture **Modern Times** *(888 Valencia St.; 415-282-9246; www.mtbs.com)* stocks a huge selection of political books and academic titles.

SHOPPING

SPAS

Even the hardiest traveler needs a break from all those hills. Spas to the rescue. The following spas provide everything from a quick dip in the hot tub to a luxurious day of self-centered bliss, from scalp massage to pedicure.

International Orange Spa Yoga Lounge

2044 Fillmore St. (2nd floor), Pacific Heights. 888-894-8811. www.internationalorange.com.

Health- and body-conscious San Franciscans rave about the aromatherapy deep-tissue massages here. Enjoy fruit and cheese on the sunny back deck. Throw in a yoga class and you'll understand what they mean by "the essence of wellness."

Kabuki Springs & Spa

1750 Geary Blvd. (at Fillmore St.), Japantown. 415-922-6000. www.kabukisprings.com.

A sojourn in this day spa will revive even the most bone-tired traveler.

Kabuki Springs & Spa

Frankie Frankeny/Kabuki Springs & Spa

Soak in the traditional Japanese baths and enjoy a full range of modern spa treatments, including ayurvedic rebalancing and seaweed wraps. Shiatsu massage is a specialty.

🎋 Nob Hill Spa

1075 California St., in the Huntington Hotel, Nob Hill. 415-345-2888. nobhillspa.com.

This 11,000sq ft sanctuary urges guests to reconnect with the gentle life. The pool, Jacuzzi and saunas will be at your disposal. Pilates and other fitness classes are offered. Treatments include packages promoting longevity (six hours of full-body treatments, including lunch); serenity (three hours of spa access, plus a massage or facial), and harmony (a romantic night of side-by-side massages, followed by a candlelight dinner catered by the hotel's Big Four restaurant).

Spa Claremont

41 Tunnel Rd., Berkeley. 510-843-3000 or 800-551-7266. www.claremontresort.com.
Buy a spa package at this historic Berkeley resort complex—it's been open since 1915—and you basically get the run of the place for a day: health club, lounge, outdoor swimming pools, steam room, sauna and fitness classes— all yours to enjoy. That's on top of your individualized treatments: massages, facials, manicures, pedicures. Lunch is included. Come on a weekday, when the facilities are less crowded.

77 Maiden Lane Salon and Spa

77 Maiden Lane (Suite 2), Union Square. 415-391-7777. www.77maidenlane.com.

Though it's a favorite among style-conscious celebrities, 77 Maiden Lane doesn't have the uppity pretenses of some high-end spas. The aim here is to make you look and feel gorgeous. For the travel weary, a short, simple massage might do the trick—prices are surprisingly reasonable. Luxury packages run four to eight hours and include a bit of everything: mud bath, massage, loofah scrub, pedicure, manicure, hair cut/color, makeup, or some combination thereof. There's even a "tune-up" for men.

Tru Spa

750 Kearny St., in the Hilton San Francisco Financial District. 415-399-9700. www.truspa.com.

This modern day spa offers stimulating oxygen facials, body massages featuring colored light therapy, and signature treatments in the Tropical Rain Forest Room (complete with jungle mist, tropical rain, and 100-gallon a minute waterfall).

Wine Country Spas

Relaxing just seems to go hand-in-hand with the slower pace of life in the Wine Country. From luxe facilities in Napa and Sonoma to Calistoga's mineral and mud baths *(see Excursions/Wine Country)*, there's a treatment to suit every sore muscle.

Fairmont Mission Inn and Spa – *100 Boyes Blvd, Sonoma. 707-938-9000 or 866-540-4499. www.fairmont.com/sonoma.* The bathing ritual is the thing to do at this Fairmont spa, which boasts it own source of thermal mineral water. Begin with an exfoliating shower, climb into a warm mineral bath (98°F), then into a hot mineral bath (102°F), and finish with a cool shower.

Meadowood – *900 Meadowood Lane, St. Helena. 707-963-3646. www.meadowood.com.* The luxurious full-service resort *(see Hotels/Wine Country)* offers a separate spa with a pool, fitness classes, personal training and yoga instruction. If the thought of working out is too much for you, indulge in a Valley Stone Massage, in which warm basalt stones and chilled marble stones are applied to induce deep relaxation.

Auberge Spa – *180 Rutherford Hill Rd., Rutherford. 866-228-2490. www.aubergedusoleil.com.* Occupying a 7,000sq ft stucco building at the upscale Auberge du Soleil *(see Hotels/Wine Country)*, the spa incorporates the local harvest in its treatments. Try a warm grapeseed oil massage or perhaps an olive-leaf body exfoliation.

Spa Villagio – *6481 Washington St.,Yountville. 707-944-8877 or 800-351-1133. www.villagio.com.* Balance your body, mind and spirit in the Mediterranean-inspired spa at the Villagio Inn. Three-hour-plus signature experiences—named Breathe, Awaken, Shine, and Together—are performed in private suites complete with fireplaces, jetted soaking tubs, steam showers, Bose sound systems, and private terraces.

SPAS

SPORTS AND RECREATION

A mild climate promotes recreational opportunities year-round, from hiking and biking to surfing, sea kayaking, and hang-gliding. Golden Gate Park, Marin County and units of the Golden Gate National Recreation Area (GGNRA) are good places to start when seeking outdoor recreation information.

Hiking

The Bay Area is a hiker's paradise, with extensive trails exploring its valleys, scaling its peaks, tracing its coastlines and penetrating its forests. Contact the GGNRA or the San Francisco Recreation & Park Department for trail maps and information. Within the city, the **Golden Gate Promenade** (3.5mi) from Aquatic Park to Fort Point below the Golden Gate Bridge, and the **Coastal Trail** (9mi) from the Golden Gate Bridge to Fort Funston, afford lovely ocean and cityscape views.

Biking

Mountain biking is an especially popular sport among the hills and valleys of Marin County and in the Presidio and Land's End areas of San Francisco. Additionally, Golden Gate Park's main thoroughfare, John F. Kennedy Drive, is closed to automobile traffic every Sunday, making it a perfect time to explore by bike—rent bikes in the Haight or at Stow Lake, and coast westward to Ocean Beach. For Bridge views, ride from Fisherman's Wharf to the base of the Golden Gate, or across the bridge into Sausalito. Shops offering rentals and trail information include:

♦ **Avenue Cyclery – Bikes:** *756 Stanyan St. at Waller St. 415-387-3155. www.avenue cyclery.com.*

♦ **Bike and Roll – Bikes, tandems, skates:** five locations including *899 Columbus Ave., North Beach. 415-229-2000. www.bikeandroll.com.*

♦ **Blazing Saddles Bike Rentals – Bikes, tandems:** six locations including *465 Jefferson St. at Hyde St., Fisherman's Wharf. 415-202-8888. www.blazingsaddles.com.*

Lincoln Park Golf Course

Mami Miyata/SFCVB

AT&T Park

Bob Ecker/SFCVB

Golf

There are several public courses within the city of San Francisco; all rent out clubs and other equipment, and open daily from dawn to dusk.

 Lincoln Park – *34th Ave. & Clement St., Outer Richmond. 415-221-9911. 415-750-4653 to reserve tee times. www.lincolnparkgc.com.*

 Golden Gate Park Golf Course – *47th Ave. & Fulton St. 415-751-8987. www.golden gateparkgolf.com.*

 Presidio Golf Course – *300 Arguello Blvd., the Presidio. 415-561-4661. www.presidio golf.com.*

AT&T Park★★

3rd & King Sts., at the Embarcadero. 415-972-2000. www.sfgiants.com.

Baseball fans won't want to miss the opportunity to see a game in this $319 million, 40,800-seat stadium (2000), which was designed to shield players and spectators from wind and fog. If you can't make a game, ballpark tours are held daily at 10:30am and 12:30pm *($10 adults, $5 children; 415-972-2400; no tours on game days).* During the 75-minute tour you'll get to visit the clubhouse, sit in the dugout and walk on the field. At the Coca-Cola Fan Lot (on the Promenade level above the left-field bleachers), pint-sized fans can slide into home plate through pop-bottle slides and run the bases at Little Giants Field.

Windsurfing

Consistent westerly winds from March to October make San Francisco Bay a prime spot for windsurfing and kiteboarding, particularly at Crissy Field, Candlestick Point, and Lake Merced. A few organizations offer instruction and rental equipment, including the Boardsports School *(Mar–Sept only; San Francisco, San Mateo and Alameda; 415-385-1224; www.boardsportsschool.com).* Note that certification is required to rent windsurfing equipment; contact the **San Francisco Boardsailing Association** *(www.sfba.org)* for additional information.

133

RESTAURANTS

The venues listed below were selected for their ambience, location and/or value for money. Rates indicate the average cost of an appetizer, an entrée and a dessert for one person (not including tax, gratuity or beverages). Most restaurants are open daily and accept major credit cards. Call for information regarding reservations, dress code and opening hours. Restaurants listed are located in San Francisco unless otherwise noted. For a complete listing of restaurants mentioned in this guide, *see Index.*

| *Luxury* | **$$$$** over $75 | *Budget* | **$$** $25–$50 |
| *Moderate* | **$$$** $50–$75 | | **$** under $25 |

Luxury

Boulevard

$$$$ **New American**
1 Mission St., Embarcadero. 415-543-6084. www.boulevard restaurant.com.
Belle Epoque accents—mosaic tile, steel girders, a pressed tin ceiling—have transformed the 1889 Audiffred Building, whose windows frame the Bay Bridge. Chef Nancy Oakes melds American regional flavors with classic French techniques in dishes like California sea bass a la plancha, and wood-oven-roasted lamb sirloin with artichokes, asparagus and housemade mint jelly. Dessert offerings range from a chocolate angel pie to a sweet carrot cake with walnut crunch ice cream.

Chez Panisse

$$$$ **California**
1517 Shattuck Ave., Berkeley. Dinner only. Closed Sun. 510-548-5525. www.chezpanisse.com.
California cuisine was born in 1971 in this casual dining room, under the watchful eye of culinary doyenne Alice Waters. It's well worth the drive over to Berkeley to sample nightly changing four-course prix-fixe menus that (make reservations a month in advance) might include local halibut carpaccio with fava bean and Meyer lemon salsa, braised guinea hen with crispy pancetta and glazed onions, or leg of lamb roasted in the fireplace.
Upstairs the **Chez Panisse Café** (**$$$**) serves simpler fare for lunch and dinner.

Farallon

$$$$ **Seafood**
450 Post St., Union Square. 415-956-6969. www.farallon restaurant.com.
Whimsical blown-glass jellyfish chandeliers float over tables, octopus stools nestle beside kelp columns—these and other flamboyant undersea fantasies complement chef Mark Franz's seafood menu here. Wash down entrées—grilled Georges Bank diver scallops with bacon-braised chicories; New Zealand Tai snapper with lobster consommé and gnocchi—with a selection from the extensive wine list.

Main dining room, Farallon

Farallon

Fifth Floor
$$$$ **New American**
12 Fourth St., in the Hotel Palomar,
Yerba Buena Gardens. Dinner
only. Closed Sun. 415-348-1555.
fifthfloorrestaurant.com.
Now presided over by chef David
Bazirgen, the kitchen turns
out innovative seasonal fare
with Mediterranean and global
influences, like lamb loin with
roasted farro and harissa juice,
and slow-cooked squab with
black trumpet mushrooms and
house-cured pancetta. Aside from
the à la carte selection, a 6-course
chef's tasting menu ($85) is offered
nightly.

Fleur de Lys
$$$$ **New French**
777 Sutter St., Union Square.
Closed Sun & Mon. 415-673-7779.
www.fleurdelyssf.com
French-born owner Hubert Keller
adds California flair to his tasting
menus (3 courses, $72; 4 course,
$82; 5 courses, $95; vegetarian,
$72) at the romantic Fleur de
Lys. Oven-roasted venison chop

with truffled baby bok choy, filet
mignon with a Bordelaise sauce,
and sunflower-seeded sea bass
with endive and mustard fondue
represent a sampling of Keller's
artistry. For non-meat eaters, a
vegetarian tasting menu is always
an option. Renovated following a
2001 fire, the main dining room is
tented with 900 yards of custom-
printed fabric.

Gary Danko
$$$$ **Continental**
800 North Point St. at Hyde St.,
Fisherman's Wharf.
Dinner only. 415-749-2060.
www.garydanko.com.
Elegant but understated decor—
plantation shutters and soothing
earth tones—allows chef-owner
Danko's culinary creations to
take center stage. Choices reflect
seasonal ingredients: Dungeness
crab salad with grapefruit,
couscous, fennel and mint; juniper-
crusted venison with chestnut
spatzle, tangerines and cranberries;
and Lousiana butter cake with
apples and huckleberry compote.

RESTAURANTS

135

Gary Danko

A five-course tasting menu ($102) can be paired with wines for an additional charge.

Jardinière
$$$$ California-French
300 Grove St. at Franklin St., Civic Center. Dinner only. 415-861-5555. www.jardiniere.com.
Hundreds of bubbles sparkle on the domed ceiling of the Champagne Rotunda in this sophisticated restaurant, favored for pre- or post-theater dining. Chef and co-owner Traci Des Jardins may treat diners to Maine diver scallops with Meyer lemon and green garlic butter, or Watson Farm lamb with cippolini onions and Castlevetrano olives; you never know exactly what awaits you as the menu changes daily.

Masa's
$$$$ French
648 Bush St., in the Executive Hotel Vintage Court, Union Square. 415-989-7154. masarestaurant.com.
A redo in 2001 transformed this dining room into a sleek space bathed in warm brown tones with chocolate mohair banquettes,

toile-covered chairs and red silk Chinese lanterns. Diners can choose from daily tasting menus of 3 ($74) or 4 ($95) courses. Your meal might start with golden chanterelle mushroom soup with spice glazed apples, progress to Paine Farms squab with braised red cabbage and applewood-smoked bacon, and end with pear gingerbread marjolane with pear ice cream.

Moderate

Delfina
$$$ Italian
3621 18th St., Mission District. 415-552-4055. delfinasf.com.
One of the hottest tables in town, this neighborhood gem is operated by husband-and-wife team Craig Stoll and Anne Spencer. Simple food and stellar service rule in the long, narrow dining room, where chef Stoll creates comfort-food masterpieces out of the freshest seasonal ingredients.
House-made pastas may be sauced with wild nettle or Louisiana white shrimp, and Fulton Valley chicken is served with olive oil mashed potatoes and king trumpet

mushrooms. Desserts are made fresh daily—from a chocolate budino to a buttermilk panna cotta.

Empress of China
$$$ **Chinese**
838 Grant Ave., Chinatown. 415-434-1345. empressofchinasf.com.
The focal point of this sixth-floor restaurant is a central pagoda whose 30ft-diameter octagonal wooden pavilion was built by craftsmen in Taiwan and reassembled here.
You'll feast on regional Chinese dishes—Mongolian beef, Peking duck, Mongolian hundred-blossom lamb, lobster Cantonese—while enjoying the views through windows that overlook the bustling Chinatown street scene.

Fog City Diner
$$$ **American**
1300 Battery St., Embarcadero. 415-982-2000. www.fogcitydiner.com.
You'll recognize this chrome and neon landmark at the foot of Telegraph Hill by the clock over its door, which advises patrons: "Don't Worry." Inside you'll find 1930s roadside diner ambience as well

as upscale burgers and handcut truffled French fries, seared Dungeness crab cakes, hand-rolled organic parpardelle, and a crispy reddened snapper filet.

Frances
$$$ **Contemporary**
3870 17th St. 415- 621-3870. www.frances-sf.com.
Chef-owner Melissa Perello's relaxed resto has quickly become a neighborhood favorite.
The selective, daily-changing menu of contemporary California fare might feature smoked steelhead trout, ricotta gnocchi, or lamb with butter beans and artichoke.

Greens
$$$ **Vegetarian**
Fort Mason Center, Bldg. A, Marina District. 415-771-6222. www.greensrestaurant.com.
Opened in 1979 by disciples of the San Francisco Zen Center, this gourmet veggie restaurant west of Fisherman's Wharf gets much of its organic produce from the center's Green Gulch Farm in Marin County. Savor such seasonal fare as coconut risotto cakes, wild mushroom

Greens

ravioli, and broccoli di Ciccio pizza with spring onions, tomatoes, feta, fontina, and Meyer lemon gremolade, along with wonderful view of the marina with the Golden Gate Bridge in the distance. The wine list here has won national awards.

John's Grill

$$$ **American**
63 Ellis St., Union Square. 415-986-3274. www.johnsgrill.com.
The true Maltese Falcon, made famous by author and former patron Dashiell Hammet (and actor Humphrey Bogart), has been at home behind the bar here since 1908.
The grill's dark, moody interior is straight out of film noir. Signature dishes chicken Jerusalem (chicken sautéed with artichokes and mushroom in a white-wine-cream sauce) and oysters Wellington (baked in puff pastry with creamed spinach and smoky bacon) share menu space with a host of steaks and seafood.

McCormick & Kuleto's

$$$ **Seafood**
900 North Point St., Fisherman's Wharf. 415-929-1730. www.mccormickandkuletos.com.
Some of the best seafood in the wharf area is served not on the water but at this spacious and lively restaurant in Ghirardelli Square. Tables on two levels boast great bay views toward Alcatraz. In the bar area, clubby wood and Art Deco appointments prevail. There's a full oyster bar and a long list of fresh fish and shellfish, from Petrale sole and Ahi tuna to Dungeness crab and steelhead salmon, all cooked to order.

Quince

$$$ **Italian**
470 Pacific Ave. Dinner only. 415-775-8500. www.quince restaurant.com.
Chef-owner Michael Tusk is a Jersey boy, but his travels after culinary school introduced him to the rustic fare of Southern France and Italy, which provides his inspiration. He sources only the freshest products from a select network of producers, and the menu is updated nightly with original takes on Italian cuisine.

Rose Pistola

$$$ **Italian**
532 Columbus Ave., North Beach. 415-399-0499. rosepistolasf.com.
A wood-burning oven dominates the open kitchen in this bustling eatery, which won the James Beard Best New Restaurant award in 1997. The menu here echoes traditional Ligurian fare prepared by the Italian immigrants who settled in North Beach in the city's early days. Local fish and shellfish star in such dishes as cioppino (San Francisco's answer to bouillabaise) and whole Branzino bass with chickpeas, Treviso and caper-currant-pinenut relish—many of which are served family-style on large platters. In good weather, enjoy people-watching from the sidewalk tables.

The Slanted Door

$$$ **Vietnamese**
1 Ferry Building, Embarcadero. 415-861-8032. www.slanted door.com.
Recently relocated to its new digs in the renovated Ferry Building, the Slanted Door offers wonderful Vietnamese-inspired cuisine. Crowds arrive early for

MUST EAT

The Slanted Door

grapefruit and jicama salad; spring rolls stuffed with pork, shrimp and mint; fresh Dungeness crab with cellophane noodles; and crispy five-spice Liberty duck leg. Parties of seven or more can order a combination of dishes to share from the prix-fixe menu ($42/ person at lunch, $48/ person at dinner).

Zuni Café
$$$ **Mediterranean**
1658 Market St., Civic Center. Closed Mon. 415-552-2522. zunicafe.com.
Opened some 30 years ago as a southwestern restaurant, Zuni now offers hearty regional French and Italian food infused with California flavors. Classics on the ever-changing menu include the succulent brick-oven-roasted chicken and the signature Caesar salad. An eclectic clientele crowd around the copper oyster bar.

Budget

Betelnut Pejiu Wu
$$ **Asian-Fusion**
2030 Union St., Cow Hollow. 415-929-8855. www.betelnut restaurant.com.
Fashioned after a traditional Southeast Asian pejiu wu, or

Zuni Café

beer house, Betelnut serves fresh regional "street food" in a British Colonial atmosphere with overhead fans swirling beside sensuous paintings of Asian women. Popular small plates and entrees like "bein pow" firecracker chicken (with Szechuan chili and toasted almonds) tend to spicy— all the better to wash them down with a large mug of imported beer.

Café de la Presse
$$ **French**
352 Grant Avenue, Chinatown. 415-398-2680. www.cafedela presse.com.
Casual brasserie meals are served at this café and international newsstand beside Chinatown Gate. The menu features French onion soup topped with cheese, salad Niçoise, and boeuf bourguignon. A favorite of foreign residents and visitors is the espresso bar, with its tempting selection of pastries.

Fior d'Italia
$$ Northern Italian
2237 Mason Street, North Beach 415-986-1886. www.fior.com.
America's oldest Italian restaurant, this institution opened in 1886 and has faced Washington Square since 1954. Historical photos line the walls; the Tony Bennett Room honors San Francisco's favorite crooner. The extensive menu offers traditional Northern Italian fare, from minestrone and house-made pasta to beef, veal and seafood to risotto and polenta. Signature dishes include the calamari, Caesar salad, gnocchi and osso buco.

Perbacco
$$ Italian
230 California St. 415-955-0663. www.perbaccosf.com.
Northern Italian fare here highlights the dishes of Piemonte. For a quick bite, sit at the marble-topped bar, where you can wash down house-cured meats with a good selection of Italian wines by the glass. Prefer a hearty meal? House-made pastas and the likes of roasted monkfish in porcini brodo will do the trick. Perbacco's more casual sister, the eno-trattoria Barbacco, opened next door in 2010.

The Stinking Rose
$$ California-Italian
325 Columbus Ave., North Beach. 415-781-7673. www.thestinkingrose.com.
Not a place to take that first date, the Stinking Rose specializes in food redolent with garlic—lots and lots of garlic. Start with the bagna calda, garlic roasted in olive oil and butter presented in a hot skillet with bread for dipping. Forty-clove garlic chicken is roasted on the bone and served with—what else?—garlic mashed potatoes. If you really feel adventurous, try garlic ice cream for dessert. The menu notes that "Vampire Fare" can be prepared without garlic.

Swan Oyster Depot
$$ Seafood
1517 Polk St., Nob Hill. Open 8am–5:30pm. Closed Sun. 415-673-1101.
The Sancimino family has operated this tiny fish market and eatery since 1946. In the window, the day's catch stops passers-by; inside, jokes fly as shells are

Perbacco

Perbacco

shucked. Take a seat at the marble counter—it's your only option, there are no tables—and order a bowl of buttery clam chowder, a plate of cracked Dungeness crab or a platter of oysters and clams on the half-shell. Wash it down with a cold glass of San Francisco's Anchor Steam bear and you'll leave a happy camper. Don't bother bringing your credit cards; Swan's only accepts cash.

Thirsty Bear
Brewing Company
$$ **Spanish**
661 Howard St., Yerba Buena Gardens. 415-974-0905.
www.thirstybear.com.
At Thirsty Bear, dozens of cold and hot tapas plates complement eight different house-made brews on tap, which range from the lightly hopped Polar Bear Pilsner, to the nitrogen conditioned Meyer E.S.B., an extra-special bitter with a smooth caramel body and floral hop aroma. Nosh on flatbreads, bocadillos and empanadas, or try one of three different versions of paella—vegetarian, a daily special, and Valenciana, a mix of meat, seafood and vegetables on saffron rice.

Yank Sing
$$ **Chinese**
49 Stevenson St. and One Rincon Center (101 Spear St.), SoMa. Lunch only. 415-957-9300.
www.yanksing.com.
This dim sum palace wins raves for the seemingly endless array of tasty offerings that tempt diners from its rolling carts. From Cantonese spring rolls to house-roasted Peking duck to steamed shrimp dumplings and fried won tons stuffed with curried shrimp and cream cheese, you'll be hard-pressed to choose. Be forewarned if your eyes are bigger than your stomach: dim sum items are priced à la carte—the more you eat, the more you'll pay.

Molinari Delicatessen
$ **Italian**
373 Columbus Ave., North Beach. Closed Sun & major holidays. 415-421-2337.
Heady whiffs of provolone, salami and olives waft from this century-old North Beach institution. Locals pop in early to pick up handmade ravioli, tortellini, olive oils and vinegars imported from Italy. Later in the morning, meats and cheeses appear on the chopping block to feed the lunch crowd. Stop in for

RESTAURANTS

a North Beach Special (prosciutto, provolone, sun-dried tomatoes and sweet bell peppers) and picnic in Washington Square.

DINING IN THE WINE COUNTRY

French Laundry

$$$$ French
6640 Washington St., Yountville. Dinner daily; lunch Fri, Sat & Sun. 707-944-2380. www.french laundry.com.
Some argue that French Laundry—lodged in a century-old stone laundry building—is the best restaurant in the U.S. Chef Thomas Keller, masterful in the preparation of sophisticated and creative French cuisine, offers a nine-course seasonal tasting menu ($270) nightly. A sommelier matches wines on request. The price is worth it for a very special occasion. Reservations available exactly two months in advance.

Tra Vigne

$$$$ Italian
1050 Charter Oak Ave., St. Helena. Closed Mon. 707-963-4444. www.travignerestaurant.com.
Italian for "among the vines," Tra Vigne reflects founder Michael

Chiarello's desire to bring southern Italy to northern California. Depending on the season the menu might offer wood-oven–baked fig pizza, fire-roasted organic chicken with smashed cannellini beans and spring herb sauce, or sage-infused papardelle with braised rabbit ragu and wild mushrooms. The grand dining room boasts 30ft ceilings and huge windows.

Bistro Jeanty

$$$ French
6510 Washington St., Yountville. 707-944-0103. www.bistro jeanty.com.
This charming neighborhood bistro on the main street in tiny Yountville is the brainchild of chef Philippe Jeanty, formerly of Domaine Chandon. Classics like daube de boeuf (beef stew with mashed potatoes, peas and carrots), cassoulet (a hearty stew of duck confit, white beans, sausage and bacon) and moules au vin rouge (mussels steamed in red wine) will linger in your memory long after they've disappeared from your plate.
If you can't get reservations, walk-ins can sit at the communal table near the bar.

John Ash & Co.

Cafe La Haye
\$\$\$ California-Mediterranean
140 E. Napa St., Sonoma.
Dinner only. 707-935-5994.
cafelahaye.com.
Some big flavors come out of the tiny kitchen in this bistro just off Sonoma Plaza. Fresh produce, meats and cheeses from Sonoma and Napa valleys provide the ingredients for dishes such as pan-seared chicken with roasted vegetables and arugula, and hand-torn papardelle with braised pork, roasted cippolini, baby spinach and Gruyère cheese. The wine list features a good selection of local boutique wines and the dining room is decorated with work by local artists.

John Ash & Co.
\$\$\$ California
4350 Barnes Road., Santa Rosa. 707-575-7350. www.vintnersinn.com.
Surrounded by vineyards at the secluded Vintners Inn, 4mi north of Santa Rosa, chef Thomas Schmidt blends fresh seasonal ingredients to create innovative entrées, like prosciutto-wrapped pheasant breast with cornbread stuffing, caramelized Brussel sprouts and maple jus, or pumpkin ravioli with pickled mushroom and crispy sage butter. If you can't tear yourself away, you can always book one of the 44 luxurious rooms at the inn.

Mustards Grill
\$\$\$ American
7399 St. Helena Hwy. (Rte. 29), Napa. 709-944-2424.
www.mustardsgrill.com.
A long-standing Napa Valley favorite, this casual ranch-style restaurant draws winemakers and other wine industry VIPs for its fresh cuisine and a top-notch wine list. The menu ranges across American regional dishes with nods to Continental and Asian, from seared ahi tuna to barbecued baby back ribs. For starters order the sublimely thin and crispy onion rings with house-made tomato-apple ketchup.

Terra
\$\$\$ California
1345 Railroad Ave., St. Helena. Dinner only. Closed Tue. 707-963-8931. www.terrarestaurant.com.
Inside this lovely 1884 fieldstone foundry you'll find an intimate dining room with soft lighting, stone wall and warm terra-cotta floors. Chef and owner Hiro Sone crafts innovative dishes using European and Asian influences: broiled sake-marinated Alaskan black cod, foie gras tortelloni, daube of lamb shoulder with Castroville artichokes. Sone's wife, pastry chef Lissa Doumani, does wonders with the likes of tiramisù, apple almond tart and chocolate bread pudding with sun-dried cherries and crème fraîche.

Tuscany
\$\$ Italian
1005 First St., Napa. Dinner only. 707-258-1000.
Diners who can't get a table at Tra Vigne are delighted to find Tuscany in the bustling heart of Napa. The 1855 structure has been renovated with an open kitchen, where diners can watch braised Sonoma duck breast, rotisserie rabbit wrapped in pancetta, and other tempting dishes being prepared. Tiramisù or cannoli topped with warm peach compote makes a memorable end to a meal here.

HOTELS

The properties listed below were selected for their ambience, location and/or value for money. Prices reflect the average cost for a standard double room for two people (not including applicable city or state taxes). Hotels in San Francisco constantly offer special discount packages. Price ranges quoted do not reflect the hotel tax of 14%. Properties are located in San Francisco, unless otherwise specified.

Luxury	**$$$$$** over $350		*Moderate*	**$$$** 175–250
Expensive	**$$$$** 250–$350		*Budget*	**$$-$** 100–$175

Luxury

The Fairmont San Francisco
$$$$$ 591 rooms
950 Mason St., Nob Hill.
415-772-5000 or 800-441-1414.
www.fairmont.com.
This famous grand hotel atop Nob Hill survived the 1906 quake and saw the creation of the United Nations in 1945. The Fairmont's location at the intersection of San Francisco's two cable-car lines provides easy access to sightseeing. Choose from handsome rooms—recently renovated—in the original building or in a 1961 tower that offers broad views across the city. The domed **Laurel Court**

restaurant ($$$) serves regional California fare. Don't miss happy hour at the exotic Tonga Room and Hurricane Bar with its thatched umbrellas and floating live band (see Nightlife).

Four Seasons San Francisco
$$$$$ 277 rooms
757 Market St., SoMa.
415-633-3000 or 800-819-5053.
www.fourseasons.com.
Soft music and fine art envelop you as you step into the lobby of this elegant, South of Market hotel. With a great location in the Yerba Buena Arts District one block from the cable-car turnaround on Powell Street, and two blocks from Union Square,

Four Seasons San Francisco

Ed Caldwell/Four Seasons San Francisco

Mandarin Oriental San Francisco

Mandarin Oriental San Francisco

the Four Seasons pampers guests in spacious rooms with floor-to-ceiling windows, thick terry robes and down pillows.
Hotel guests have free access to the adjacent Sports Club/LA, with its 10,000sq ft gym, junior Olympic-size pool and full spa.

The Huntington Hotel
$$$$$ 136 rooms
1075 California St., Nob Hill.
415-474-5400 or 800-227-4683.
www.huntingtonhotel.com.
Overlooking Huntington Park on the California Street cable-car line, this 1924 classic started out as a luxury apartment complex. True to their origins, rooms are oversized and posh—think silk, damask, leather and velvet—fitting lodgings for the likes of former guests Luciano Pavarotti, Desmond Tutu and Paloma Picasso. Your palate will delight in New American dishes at the clubby **Big 4 Restaurant ($$$)**, and your stress will melt away after a treatment at the hotel's state-of-the-art Nob Hill Spa (see Spas).

Mandarin Oriental, San Francisco
$$$$$ 158 rooms
222 Sansome St., Financial District.
415-276-9888 or 800-622-0404.
mandarinoriental.com.
From the hotel's ground-floor entry, high-speed elevators whisk guests to their aeries, located between the 38th and 48th stories atop 345 California Center. Spectacular picture-window views await you in your room (binoculars provided), along with Egyptian cotton sheets, and your choice of cotton or terrycloth robes and slippers. If trekking up San Francisco's hills isn't enough exercise for you, try a workout in the hotel's fitness center; alternatively, purchase a $20 day pass and work out across the street at San Francisco's premier fitness center, Equinox Fitness.

Taj Campton Place
$$$$$ 110 rooms
340 Stockton St., Union Square.
415-781-5555 or 800-235-4300.
www.camptonplace.com.
An intimate hotel popular in a former incarnation with the

HOTELS

white-gloved "carriage trade" set, Campton Place is the epitome of elegance and fine service. Pear wood paneling and cozy window seats make up elements of the peaceful uncluttered decor, while insulated glass filters out noise from nearby Union Square. Splurge on vibrant Mediterranean cuisine at **Taj Campton Place Restaurant ($$$$)**—you can work it off later at the 9th-floor fitness center.

Expensive

Hotel Monaco
$$$$ 201 rooms
501 Geary St., Theater District.
415-292-0100 or 866-622-5284.
www.monaco-sf.com.
This 1910 Beaux-Arts classic offers high-style comfort in a convenient location a few blocks from Union Square. Baroque-style plaster fireplaces and sumptuous armchairs invite lobby conversation. In the guest rooms, Provençal fabrics drape over canopy beds and Chinese-inspired furnishings lend an exotic look. Housed in the former ballroom, now restored with Art Deco details, the stunning **Grand Café ($$$)** offers bistro-style meals. Your four-legged friends are welcome here, but if you can't bring Fido, ask for a goldfish to keep you company.

Hotel Palomar
$$$$ 195 rooms
12 Fourth St., SoMa.
415-348-1111 or 866-373-4941.
www.hotelpalomar-sf.com.
The Kimpton Group's top-of-the-line venture embraces the fifth through ninth floors of a post-

quake, 1908 landmark building at the corner of Market Street. Tailored lines, geometric carpeting and bright persimmon accents offer contemporary elegance throughout. Guests have access to 24-hour onsite fitness center and in-room spa services. The acclaimed **Fifth Floor restaurant ($$$$)** serves New American cuisine with a Mediterranean influence (*see Must Eat*).

Westin San Francisco Market Street
$$$$ 676 rooms
50 Third St., 415-974-6400.
www.westinsf.com.
Formerly the Argent Hotel, this property was recently rebranded and renovated to elegant success. All rooms feature stunning city skyline views through floor-to-ceiling windows, contemporary decor, and feather pillows. Dine on Northern Italian inspired cuisine at the lobby level **Ducca ($$$)**.

Westin St. Francis
$$$$ 1,253 rooms
335 Powell St., Union Square.
415-397-7000 or 800-Westin 1.
www.westinstfrancis.com.
See Landmarks.
Occupying a Renaissance- and Baroque-revival structure built in 1904, this landmark hotel facing Union Square is renowned for its legendary service.
A historic charm still pervades the rooms in the main building with their Empire-style furnishings; more contemporary rooms with large bay windows and dramatic city views occupy the 32-story tower built in 1972. All are outfitted with Westin's signature Heavenly Bed™.

Clift

$$$$ **363 rooms**

495 Geary St. 415-775-4700 or
800-697-1791. www.clifthotel.com.
Dark meets light, antique goes
modern, and eccentric cajoles
conservative at this high-style
hostelry. Built in 1913 and
reconceived for the 21st century by
Philippe Starck, it features elegantly
sleek public areas and guestrooms
swathed in quiet tones of foggy
gray, beige and lavender. The
legendary Redwood Room lounge
features original 1933 paneling and
a long bar carved from a single tree.

Argonaut

$$$$ **252 rooms**

495 Jefferson St.
415-563-0800 or 866-415-0704.
www.argonauthotel.com.
Perfectly located near Ghirardelli
Square, the cable-car turnaround
and Fisherman's Wharf, this
maritime-themed hotel occupies
a 1907 waterfront warehouse at
The Cannery. Some rooms offer
views of the bay and Alcatraz; all
are well soundproofed and have
modern amenities, including flat-
screen TVs, CD–DVD players and
complimentary high-speed
Internet access.

InterContinental San Francisco

$$$$ **550 rooms**

54 Fourth St. 415-986-4400
or 800-227-3804. www.inter
continentalsanfrancisco.com.
San Francisco's newest
InterContinental hotel rose on the
scene in February 2008, piercing
the SoMa skyline with its 32-story
blue-glass tower.
With LEED Gold certification, the
modern hotel's boasts numerous
eco-friendly features, including
floor-to-ceiling windows, organic
toiletries, and automatic sensors
on lights, sinks and toilets.
A state-of-the-art gym and an
indoor infinity-edge lap pool with
skylights are both located on the
6th floor, along with the 10-room
I-Spa. Off the lobby, Luce restaurant
features Tuscan cuisine.

Argonaut Hotel

Markham Johnson/Argonaut Hotel

HOTELS

Moderate

Commodore Hotel

$$$ **110 rooms**

825 Sutter St., Union Square.
415-923-6800 or 800-338-6848.
www.thecommodorehotel.com.

Hippest of the hip Joie de Vivre
group, the Commodore is an
offbeat urban oasis of neo-
Deco styling. Whimsical custom
furnishings, 1920s luxury-liner
detailing and dramatic murals
create an air of the unexpected.
The colorful diner-like Titanic
Café serves breakfast and lunch;
the hypnotic Red Room lounge
(it really is completely red!) stays
open late for martini lovers.

Executive Hotel Vintage Court

$$$ **107 rooms**

650 Bush St., Union Square.
415-392-4666 or 1-888-388-3932.
executivehotels.net/sanfrancisco.

This Euro-style property creates
a cozy atmosphere in its lobby,
where guests gather Tue–Sat
evenings to enjoy wine and
cocktails. Decorated in a palette
of soft greens and cream, rooms
are named after local wineries,
and invite relaxation with fluffy
duvets and down pillows.
Room rates hover at the lower
end of the price range ($199-$229)
to ($139-$250).
Adjacent to the hotel, **Masa's**
(**$$$$**) constantly wins raves for
its contemporary French cuisine
(*see Restaurants*).

The Handlery Union Square Hotel

$$$ **377 rooms**

351 Geary St., Union Square.
415-781-7800 or 800-995-4874.
www.handlery.com.

A family operation that opened in
1948 (on the site of a 1907 hotel),
The Handlery is an elegantly
traditional, European-style hotel
centrally located on Union Square.
Renovated in 2010, rooms now
feature luxury bedding and flat-
panel TVs. Perhaps the property's
most noteworthy feature, the
heated outdoor swimming pool is
a mid-city rarity.

Hotel Bohème

$$$ **15 rooms**

444 Columbus Ave., North Beach.
415-433-9111. www.hotel
boheme.com.

Reflecting the bohemian tastes of
the Beat Generation in 1950s San
Francisco, this quaint boutique
hotel at the foot of Telegraph Hill
is dedicated to the spirit of Jack
Kerouac, Lawrence Ferlinghetti
and their cohorts. Cozy rooms
with burnt orange walls occupy
a three-story building erected in
the 1880s. The courteous staff is
glad to help make reservations for
restaurants, theater and tours.

Hotel Diva

$$$ **111 rooms**

440 Geary St., Union Square.
415-885-0200 or 800-553-1900.
hoteldiva.com.

The glitziest of several moderately
priced San Francisco hotels in
the Personality Hotels group,
the trendy Diva is a polished
Euro-tech hotel. Located in the
Theater District, and popular

MUST STAY

with visiting members of the film industry, the property offers sleek contemporary rooms accented with sculptured steel headboards, cobalt-blue carpeting, modern black leather couches and bright orange shower curtains. Amenities include flat-screen TVs, Sharper Image iPod alarm clocks, a 24-hour fitness room and a complimentary wine hour.

Hotel Juliana
$$$ **107 rooms**
590 Bush St., Nob Hill.
415-392-2540 or 866-325-9457.
www.julianahotel.com.
Bold, bright and stylish in its decor, this nine-story boutique property at the foot of Nob Hill retains an intimate atmosphere in a 1903 building. The hotel packs in a lot of extras for the price: pillowtop beds, Aveda toiletries, a complimentary wine reception each evening, and weekday morning sedan service to the Financial District. There's a workout facility on-site, and your four-legged friends are welcome here.

Hotel Rex
$$$ **94 rooms**
562 Sutter St., Union Square.
415-433-4434 or 800-433-4434.
www.thehotelrex.com.
The redesign of this historic boutique hotel follows the theme of the literary and arts salons rife in San Francisco in the 1920s and 30s. Quotes from regional authors adorn the walls of different floors. Sunny colors brighten the guest rooms, which are accented with hand-painted lampshades. With its dark paneling, comfortable seating and shelves of antiquarian books, the Rex's lobby has the feel of a gentleman's study.

Hotel Triton
$$$ **140 rooms**
342 Grant Ave., Chinatown.
415-394-0500 or 800-800-1299.
www.hoteltriton.com.
Standard fare certainly doesn't apply at this avant-garde boutique hotel facing Chinatown Gate, where the eye-popping room decor was designed by a group of local artists. With lodgings like Eco Rooms (all-natural linens, biodegradable toiletries), Zen Dens (bamboo plants, images of goddess Tara) and celebrity suites dedicated to the likes of Jerry Garcia, Häagen Dazs and Kathy Griffin, the Triton is wonderfully eclectic. Custom armoires hide Sony flat-screen TVs, which, of course, include the 24-hour Yoga channel. All this and they're pet-friendly, too.

The Inn at the Opera
$$$ **48 rooms**
333 Fulton St., Civic Center.
415-863-8400 or 800-325-2708.
This elegant small hotel is popular among musicians and stage performers, owing to its location a block from the War Memorial Opera House (the stars often choose the Symphony or Opera suites). Tastefully decorated rooms include refrigerators, wet bar areas and microwaves for après-theater snacking. Intimate and romantic, the delightful **Ovation ($$)** restaurant serves traditional French fare.

Hotel Frank
$$$ 153 rooms
386 Geary St., Union Square.
415-986-2000 or 877-828-4478.
hotelfranksf.com.
Built in 1908 but restored in Art
Deco style, this chic boutique
hotel offers bold, stylish décor—
eye-catching houndstooth-
patterned carpeting, emerald
green headboards in a crocodile
print, and whimsical glass light
fixtures. New York deli-style fare
is available from **Max's on the
Square ($$)**, and Wi-Fi access is
complementary.

Mark Hopkins InterContinental
$$$ 380 rooms
*One Nob Hill 415-392-3434 or 877-
270-1390. www.intercontinental
markhopkins.com.*
Opened in 1926 on the crest of Nob
Hill, this grand, historic hotel stands
on the site of the former mansion
of "Big Four" Mark Hopkins.
Elegantly traditional rooms feature
a rich palate of golden yellows and
sienna, dark woods and marble
bathrooms with black granite
vanities. The 19th floor's legendary
Top of the Mark lounge supplies
sweeping views and a 100
Martinis menu.

The Palace Hotel
$$$ 553 rooms
*2 New Montgomery St., Financial
District. 415-512-1111 or 800-
325-3589. www.sfpalace.com.*
A Market Street landmark
since 1875, The Palace—now a
Starwood hotel—bridges the gap
between the 19C and the 21C.
Renovated from head to toe in
1991, the Palace shines again with
its centerpiece, the sumptuous
Garden Court. Decked out with
marble pillars, stained-glass
domed ceiling and Austrian
crystal chandeliers, the Garden
Court has hosted many a VIP
event over the years. Luxurious
rooms, decorated in tones of
soft blue, cream and yellow, are
appointed with 14ft ceilings,
marble baths, down comforters
and windows that open. Next to
the heated indoor lap pool are a
whirlpool and eucalyptus sauna.

Sir Francis Drake Hotel
$$$ 417 rooms
450 Powell St., Union Square.
415-392-7755 or 800-795-7129.
www.sirfrancisdrake.com.
Named for the English explorer
who sailed into the area in 1579,
the Drake was the city's most
opulent luxury hotel when
it opened in 1928. That air of
grandeur still rules today, evident
in the doorman in Beefeater
costume and in the sumptuous
lobby, with its marble staircase,
crystal chandeliers and gold-leaf
ceiling. Resting on the cable-car
line one block from Union Square,
the hotel's 21st-floor penthouse
holds one of San Francisco's most
longstanding nightclubs, **Harry
Denton's Starlight Room** (*see
Nightlife*).

Stanyan Park Hotel
$$$ 16 rooms
750 Stanyan St., Haight-Ashbury.
*415-751-1000. www.stanyan
park.com.*
Overlooking Golden Gate Park
on the west end of bohemian
Haight Street, this three-story
1905 Victorian house rates

Sir Francis Drake Hotel

Cris Molina/Sir Francis Drake Hotel

inclusion on the National Register of Historic Places. Tasteful rooms, are decorated with period furnishings—Victorian, of course—and feature sitting areas, color cable TVs, full baths and free WiFi. Reasonable rates include continental breakfast and afternoon tea.

Washington Square Inn

$$$ 15 rooms
1660 Stockton St., North Beach.
415-981-4220 or 800-388-0220.
www.wsisf.com.

A charming and intimate European-style inn at the foot of Telegraph Hill in the heart of bohemian North Beach, this lovely bed-and-breakfast is proud of its highly personalized service. Individually decorated rooms feature French antiques, fresh orchids and robes; some have sitting area and fireplaces. Rates include afternoon tea, evening wine and hors-d'oeuvres, and a continental breakfast either delivered to your room or served downstairs at the antique table overlooking the square.

Budget

Andrews Hotel

$$ 48 rooms
624 Post St., Union Square.
415-563-6877 or 800-926-3739.
www.andrewshotel.com.

This bright and cozy Victorian inn offers intimacy and personal service in the European style, three blocks off Union Square. Rooms sport pastel colors and floral prints and are equipped with small TVs and DVD players (complimentary movies are available at the front desk). Each morning, a complimentary continental breakfast—breads, seasonal fruits, coffee, tea—is delivered to the landing on each floor. In the evening, enjoy a glass of California wine—on the house—at Fino restaurant.

HOTELS

Chancellor Hotel

$$ **137 rooms**
433 Powell St., Union Square.
415-362-2004 or 800-428-4748.
www.chancellorhotel.com.
Location is everything at this
European-style 15-story inn,
opened in 1914 on the Powell-
Hyde and Powell-Mason cable-car
lines, right on Union Square.
One of the city's best bargains,
the Chancellor boasts amenities
like in-room safes, a pillow menu
(choose your favorite style), and an
on-site restaurant (**Luques**), that
you'd expect from a higher-priced
property. Guests have free access
to the health club at the Westin St.
Francis, a mere half-block away.

Grant Plaza Hotel

$$ **72 rooms**
465 Grant Ave., Chinatown.
415-434-3883 or 800-472-6899.
www.grantplaza.com.
A remarkable value in the heart of
Chinatown, this clean, bright inn
may be simple, but it offers such
modern conveniences as data
ports, hair dryers and electronic
key cards. Rooms have color TVs
and private baths. The cable car to
Fisherman's Wharf is just a block
away, and Union Square shopping
is an easy three-block stroll from
the hotel.

Hotel Beresford

$$ **114 rooms**
635 Sutter St., Union Square.
415-673-9900 or 800-533-6533.
www.beresford.com.
This pleasant, family-run hotel
attracts British visitors with its
Victorian decor and its English
pub, the White Horse Tavern.
Rooms are small, but nicely
furnished in dark woods and

pastels. Rates include a basic
continental breakfast. The
property's similarly priced sister
hotel, the **Hotel Beresford Arms**
*(701 Post St.; 415-673-2600; 102
rooms)*, is three blocks away.

Hotel Bijou

$$ **65 rooms**
111 Mason St., Union Square.
415-771-1200 or 800-771-1022.
www.hotelbijou.com.
Located a block away from cable-
car stops, the Art Deco-style Bijou
recalls a 1920s movie palace;
on its walls hang photos of San
Francisco's old movie houses.
Bright, jewel-toned guest rooms
are named for films shot in the
city, which are illustrated in each
room by original still photographs.
Double features of San Francisco-
based films are screened nightly
in the small lobby theater.
Rates include a complimentary
continental breakfast.

Nob Hill Hotel

$$ **50 rooms**
835 Hyde St., Nob Hill.
415-885-2987 or 877-662-4455.
www.nobhillhotel.com.
Restored in 1998, this
neighborhood gem—which
dates from 1906—has reclaimed
its original marble flooring,
alabaster chandeliers and
stained-glass windows. Cozy
rooms sport Victorian furnishings
and objets d'art, iron beds and
velvet comforters, along with
mini refrigerators, microwaves
and coffee makers. The hotel's
Colombini Bistro ($$$) specializes
in Italian cuisine.

San Remo Hotel

$ 62 rooms

2237 Mason St., North Beach.
415-776-8688 or 800-352-7366.
www.sanremohotel.com.

Simplicity rules here: like a European pension, all rooms in the San Remo share baths, and none have phones or TVs. Cozy accommodations are neatly kept and pretty, furnished with late-19C antiques. Ask the friendly, helpful staff to direct you to popular sights, such as Fisherman's Wharf, which lie within easy walking distance.

WINE COUNTRY HOTELS

Luxury

Auberge du Soleil

$$$$$ 50 rooms

180 Rutherford Hill Rd., Rutherford.
707-963-1211 or 800-348-5406.
www.aubergedusoleil.com.

The breezy terrace of this upscale country inn offers the wine-weary traveler an unparalleled view across the Napa Valley. Accommodations consist mainly of one- and two-bedroom suites tucked into the

Auberge du Soleil

Auberge du Soleil

hillside overlooking the 33 acres of silvery olive trees that surround the property. While you're here, sample Mediterranean-inspired cuisine at the **Restaurant at Auberge du Soleil ($$$$)**, and pamper yourself with a Napa-themed treatment at the **Auberge Spa** (*see Spas*)

Meadowood Napa Valley

$$$$$ 85 rooms

900 Meadowood Lane, St. Helena.
707-963-3646 or 800-458-8080.
www.meadowood.com.

A perfect perch for Wine Country adventures, this world-class resort

Meadowood Napa Valley

Meadowood Napa Valley

Wine Country Junior Suite,
Fairmont Sonoma Mission Inn & Spa

Fairmont Hotels and Resorts

off Napa's Silverado Trail offers top-flight service. Exquisite grounds encompass rustic cottages set in a wooded grove; rooms feature private terraces and stone fireplaces. Between golf, tennis, the full-service spa, and the wine center (whose staff can arrange tastings and vineyard picnics), it would be easy never to leave the property. Don't miss innovative Wine Country cuisine at the superb **Restaurant at Meadowood ($$$$)**.

Expensive

Fairmont Sonoma Mission Inn & Spa
$$$$ 228 rooms
100 Boyes Blvd, Boyes Hot Springs.
707-938-9000 or 800-257-7544.
www.sonomamissioninn.com.
This early-20C resort just outside the town of Sonoma achieved fame long before spas became endemic. Inside pink stucco walls and Mission-style architecture, every modern touch prevails, from high-tech phones to aromatherapy wraps. Rooms in the historic

main building, decorated with pine furnishings, ceiling fans and plantation shutters, were restored in early 2004. The grounds include an 18-hole golf course, and the spa (see Spas) boasts its own on-site source of thermal mineral water. **Santé ($$$)** is renowned for its California cuisine.

Honor Mansion
$$$$ 13 rooms
891 Grove St., Healdsburg.
707-433-4277 or 800-554-4667.
www.honormansion.com.
Luxury awaits you behind the door of this restored 1883 house, where owners Cathi and Steve Fowler have anticipated their guests' nearly every need in individually decorated rooms and suites. Four lovely vineyard suites out back spell romance with gas fireplaces and private patios with your own outdoor whirlpool. Rates (rooms start at $200) include a rich multicourse breakfast that will prepare you for a long day of wine tasting. Ask the helpful staff to arrange for wine tours.

Villagio Inn & Spa

$$$$ **112 rooms**

6481 Washington St., Yountville.
707-944-8877 or 800-351-1133.
www.villagio.com.

Reminiscent of a Tuscan village—
with two-story villas surrounding
lush gardens and vineyards,
fountains and waterways,
swimming pools and tennis
courts—the Villagio combines its
resort atmosphere with a health
spa (see Spas). In the rooms, warm
tones are accented by wood-
burning fireplaces. Amenities
include a welcome bottle of wine,
whirlpool bathtubs and private
decks and patios.

Villagio's older sister, the lovely
Vintage Inn ($$$$), is right up
the street *(6541 Washington St.;*
707-944-1112 or 800-351-1133;
www.vintageinn.com).

Moderate

El Bonita Motel

$$$ **41 rooms**

195 Main St., St. Helena.
707-963-3216 or 800-541-3284.
www.elbonita.com.

Located in the heart of the
delightful town of St. Helena,
this roadside motel offers clean,
comfortable rooms decked
out with such conveniences as
kitchenettes, irons and ironing
boards and hairdryers; some
rooms even have whirlpool
baths. Stroll the gardens or take
a dip in the swimming pool. If
weather permits, you can enjoy
your complimentary continental
breakfast outside on the patio.

Sonoma Hotel

$$$ **16 rooms**

110 W. Spain St., Sonoma.
707-996-2996 or 800-468-6016.
www.sonomahotel.com.

From the stone fireplace in the
lobby to the claw-foot tubs,
twig nightstands and rustic iron
headboards in the cozy guest
rooms, this hotel oozes country
charm. It was built in 1880 on the
northwest corner of Sonoma's
town square as a dry-goods store
and community center. Guests are
treated to a continental breakfast
each morning and a wine tasting
in the lobby each evening. The
hotel's restaurant, **the girl & the
fig ($$$)**, characterizes its fine fare
as "country food with a French
passion. The **late-night brasserie**
menu **($$)** is available until 11pm
Fri–Sat.

Budget

Hotel La Rose

$$ **47 rooms**

308 Wilson St., Santa Rosa.
707-579-3200 or 800-527-6738.
www.hotellarose.com.

Rooms in the original stone
structure (1907), on Railroad
Square in the heart of Santa Rosa's
historic district, are individually
outfitted with American and
European antiques as well as
modern amenities such as large-
screen TVs. Ask for a room in the
newer Carriage House across
the street; second-floor rooms
here have 15ft peaked windows
and French doors opening onto
balconies that overlook a garden
courtyard.

HOTELS

SAN FRANCISCO

The following abbreviations may appear in this Index: NHP National Historic Park; **NHS** National Historic Site; **NRA** National Recreation Area; **SHP** State Historic Park; **SP** State Park.

INDEX